THE PRESIDING GENIUS
OF THE PLACE

Bill Grogan, master teacher, at work in the mid-1960s.

THE PRESIDING GENIUS OF THE PLACE

HOW BILL GROGAN TRANSFORMED LIVES, ORGANIZATIONS, AND HIGHER EDUCATION

Allison Chisolm

Worcester Polytechnic Institute
Worcester, Massachusetts

Copyright © 2016 by Worcester Polytechnic Institute

Design by TidePool Press
Printed in the United States by Thomson-Shore

Worcester Polytechnic Institute
100 Institute Road, Worcester, MA 01609-2280
www.wpi.edu

Library of Congress Cataloging-in-Publication Data

Chisolm, Allison 1962-

    The Presiding Genius of the Place: How Bill Grogan Transformed Lives,
        Organizations, and Higher Education
    p.cm.
    ISBN: 978-0-692-66881-8
    1. Grogan, William R. ("Bill"), 1924-2015 2. Worcester (Mass.)—Biography
    3. Education—History 4. Worcester Polytechnic Institute—History
    5. Education—Engineering 6. Higher Education—Reform
    7. Management—Managing Change 8. Phi Kappa Theta—History
    9. U.S. Navy—History
    I. Title.

2016935983

DEDICATION

To Peter, for patiently waiting

CONTENTS

WILLIAM ROBERT GROGAN   College Preparatory

"The presiding genius of the place"

Wee Willie, the wonderful wizard, works with "wim and wigor." Will willing-
ly works with witty wisdom whenever work warrants winning. Yes, this is Bill,
alias "Professor", alias "Doctor" Grogan. His leadership in studies and in
extra-curricular activities has earned him these honorary degrees from the University of Lee High and all the members therein. In addition to his already long
list of achievements, Bill could be called a director-playwright, for he has written
and directed a number of skits for the class during his four-year stay. His out-
of-school work falls into two types, the first of which is his job as Lee sports reporter for the "Berkshire Evening Eagle." The other finds Bill as an inventor
of some means. Although his inventions have not been put to any particular
usage, they supply much comedy for onlookers. Either in or out of school Bill
can be distinguished as a short boy riding astride giant-sized steps. It is often
wondered what his hurry is, but we all know that Bill, hurry or not, will reach his
goal and remain on top.

Class President 2-3-4, Ferncliff Echo Staff 1-2-3-4, Editor-in-Chief 4, De-
bating Club 1-2-3-4, Echo Party 1-2-3-4, Freshman Party Decorating
Committee 3, "June Mad" 3, Ring Committee 3, Radio Play 3, Prom
Committee 3, Class Basketball 3, Chairman Forum 3-4, Freshman
Party 4, Hallowe'en Party 4, Announcement Committee 4, Pro Merito,
Commencement Speaker.

Bill's high school record hints strongly at the notable career that lay ahead.

THE PRESIDING GENIUS
OF THE PLACE

THE WPI PLAN was a bold experiment. How could a highly respected, well-established engineering school replace all required courses for all students in all majors with a program having no required courses, projects as major degree requirements, and a strong humanities component? And could it do so while maintaining educational quality and retaining professional accreditation, and still not miss a beat in preparing students for productive careers?

The decision to change WPI's educational philosophy, degree requirements, and academic operations was voluntary. There was no immediate crisis for institutional survival. Still, the consequences of failure were enormous. No college faculty had ever gambled the future of their school and so many careers on an untested experiment like this.

William R. Grogan, who helped design the experiment, was chosen to manage its changes and achieve its visionary educational goals during the early tumultuous years. The result was the creation of a world-recognized, premier technological education program founded on project-based learning.

While this accomplishment alone would be the highlight of any career, it represents only one aspect of the breadth of Bill Grogan. Here are some others:

- As an officer in the Navy Reserve, he patriotically served his country during two wars and gave significant advisory service to the Navy Department after that.

- As an engineer, he produced quality works that resulted in patents for technical innovations and significant management improvements for companies with which he was associated.
- In the community, his many associations included updating education practices in the Worcester Diocese of the Catholic Church.
- On campus, he permanently influenced social life through his seventy years of local and national service to Phi Kappa Theta fraternity.
- And in the classroom, he offered a one-of-a-kind learning experience to students who were fortunate enough to take his classes.

In all these ways, Bill influenced the lives of many thousands of individuals—directly, through his wise counsel, and indirectly, with the outcomes of his achievements. Few individuals have earned the admiration, respect, and love he engendered during his lifetime.

This book tells Bill's story. Although it can capture only the tip of the iceberg, it does paint a compelling picture of this remarkable man.

And what kind of man was he? He was a genial soul who connected with people in all walks of life. He was a visionary who managed change: change that improved the lives of those around him, and also those who never knew him but who will long benefit from products of his exceptional vision.

I hope you enjoy this glimpse into an extraordinary life.

Robert W. Fitzgerald '53
Professor Emeritus, Civil and
Environmental Engineering
and Fire Protection Engineering

The Many Sides of Bill Grogan

He wasn't very tall, but he had an outsized personality that pulled people to him and persuaded them to adopt his viewpoint. If he was in a dining room, at some point in the evening everyone's attention would turn to him. He had a lot of stories to share, often accompanied by an instructive lesson or two.

Some called him "the little man with a hammer." To others, he was "Dean Grogan" or "Brother Grogan." Earlier in life he was "Billy"; in high school he was known as "Wee Willie." And long before he joined the WPI faculty, his friends nicknamed him "Professor." On military duty, he was Ensign, and then Lieutenant Grogan.

No matter which name they knew him by, Bill Grogan made people feel that they were his particularly good friends. This was his special skill, a fact made clear by the hundreds of people who felt that they could claim this special status.

With so many facets, it's difficult to represent the one "true" Bill Grogan. There are many versions of his story, and the ones he shared changed over time. It has been my challenge to reflect his multiple personas, undergirded by the endless supply of love and respect that so many people had for him throughout his 90 years on this Earth.

May you find the Bill you remember with fondness; may you learn from the Bill you never knew.

—AC

CHAPTER ONE

The Olive in the Neck of the Bottle

Progress comes from the respectful friction of good ideas.
—Fran Harvey '37

SIX HOURS OF drafting lessons every week. With pencils and India ink. And drafting tools little changed from those used by WPI's first students a hundred years earlier, when the school was called the Worcester County Free Institute of Industrial Science.

These weekly lessons were traditionally useful to train mechanical engineers to draw everything from machine parts to full manufacturing systems. Engineering drawing in the fall, followed by descriptive geometry the next semester, were important skills for students to record precise measurements and perspectives on paper before making any models or actual machinery.

But for chemical, civil, and electrical engineers—not to mention students in chemistry, mathematics, management engineering, and physics (who collectively just managed to outnumber the mechanical engineers at WPI by the mid-1960s)—these lessons represented time lost

Above: *Leighton Wellman teaches engineering drawing in the time-honored way.*

I

to the pursuit of other academic subjects. Precision of thought is what they sought, and course options offering a different sort of perspective.

Those six hours were what Bill Grogan referred to as "the olive in the neck of the bottle." And while it may not have been apparent at the time, the battle over that seemingly mundane requirement would be the spark that ignited a far larger educational revolution at WPI.

First as a student and then as a professor of electrical engineering at WPI, Bill had little patience for his mechanical engineering colleagues who insisted that the requirement was essential for all students.

If the school could liberate those six hours a week, a whole new curricular world could open up for WPI's students. For starters, they could have more than two electives during their entire four-year undergraduate education. And they could gain a wider awareness of subjects outside their major, or even outside the confines of the campus, set on a hill above industrial Worcester.

By 1966, when WPI's president asked him to head a curriculum study committee, Professor William R. Grogan '46 had been on the WPI faculty for 20 years. This was his chance to pluck out the olive and release new ideas to broaden the educational role of the college he loved. To update a century of tradition and prepare students for an era of rapid technological changes. To extend and deepen the intellectual influence of the Institute.

Bill would go on to make this his life's work.

When his committee's first report came out in February 1967, proposing that drawing courses become electives for freshmen, most faculty in the tradition-bound Mechanical Engineering Department voiced their strong opposition to the changes.

"They were the keepers of this mechanical drawing requirement," Bill later told his friend and fellow faculty member Rick Vaz '79, "and there was a whole stable of faculty members whose job it was to do nothing but teach mechanical drawing to these poor freshmen who didn't want to take it."

Not just faculty members bent Bill's ear. He even heard from several faculty wives lobbying their case, asking him, "Why are you doing this?

You're going to cost my husband his job."

Despite this opposition, Bill firmly believed that WPI needed to create more flexibility in the curriculum to make room for innovation. Taking on the drawing requirement was a convenient distraction for the magician who wanted far more radical changes. He thought students should put down their T-squares and drawing boards and strike out on an individual curricular path that would prepare them for responsibility and competent leadership in a rigorous profession that increasingly demanded imagination as well as technical ability.

Editors at the student newspaper, *Tech News*, feared the faculty would vote down the new curriculum. In the issue published the day before the faculty vote, they encouraged students to share their views with their professors and "make some constructive noise." If the opposition won, their editorial said, "the tragedy is that it may be the result of petty jealousies, selfish protection of individual interests, and an uninformed disregard for a well-documented body of enlightened recommendations."

Bill knew he needed every vote he could muster. As he later told Vaz, he walked over to the Physical Education Department, "which at the time had full-time faculty with voting rights, but they would normally never attend the faculty meetings and would never vote," Vaz recalled. Bill asked athletic director Bob Pritchard, "What will it take to get you and all your people to come over and vote for this thing?" And he said, "We would want your promise, that as long as you had anything to do with it, WPI would continue to have a physical education requirement."

As Vaz told the story, "A deal was struck. They showed up. They voted. It passed. And to this day, WPI has a physical education requirement and not many other schools do."

On April 20, 1967, the faculty gathered for a late afternoon meeting in Morgan Hall. The Executive Committee, consisting of the engineering department heads and the dean of the faculty, sat at the head table. It recommended that the faculty support the new freshman-sophomore curriculum.

The vote was a clear mandate, 82 to 27. WPI faculty members had put aside their individual concerns to overwhelmingly support extensive changes to the curriculum. Beyond approving the curriculum study committee's proposal, the faculty also voted unanimously to adopt a minors program in the humanities and social sciences, and beyond the committee's report, to accept some 40 other changes in departmental curricula across the school.

The student paper heralded "great foresight on the part of the faculty and administration in planning for a future in which the engineer and scientist must also be the humanitarian and philosopher."

On May 18, 1967, the faculty gathered again and voted on the curriculum committee's second report, approving bachelor of science degree programs in economics, business management, and the humanities.

The olive was out. And having shown that an empowered faculty, given the freedom to innovate and the support of the administration, could bring about much-needed change, WPI had taken a small but essential first step toward what would become a revolutionary redesign of engineering education. "If we could make that seemingly minor change in programming, but one with enormous philosophical implications, anything seemed possible," Bill told WPI's alumni magazine in 1996.

After the faculty votes of 1967, Bill Grogan readily acknowledged that "there are many problems that need to be worked out concerning these programs." Over the next three years, and during many late-night committee meetings, he would have the chance to help tackle them in a far more comprehensive way, leading to yet another critical faculty vote.

For despite the progress the curriculum committee brought about, greater flexibility in course selection didn't translate into greater numbers of applicants. WPI remained a tuition-dependent institution. More radical change was needed to set the private school apart from its less-expensive state university counterparts.

Starting in 1968 a presidentially appointed faculty planning group, and then in June 1969 an elected committee of faculty members, including Grogan, developed what came to be known as the WPI Plan. It proposed to eliminate all course requirements to encourage students to determine their own course of study, which would include the

4

completion of two real-world projects: one in their major and a second in which they might examine the intersection of technology and society.

As before, many faculty members felt threatened by the changes. "A number of the older faculty do not really see their place in the program," wrote chemical engineering professor Alvin Weiss in response to the Planning Committee's proposal. "The committee has generated feelings that it wants take a quantum jump, to even take a risk," he warned. "Engineers do not work this way." Many argued for some kind of compromise; a trial phase, perhaps, rather than an all-or-nothing overhaul.

By October 1969, even WPI's trustees, known at the time for their rigid thinking and political inclination toward the far right, supported the need for change. According to Howard Freeman '40, the shift started with a discussion about Abbie Hoffman. Learning the local-born anarchist would be returning to Worcester that month, WPI students had invited the Chicago Seven member to speak on campus. The subject prompted more than a little discussion among the board members, Freeman said.

"Bob Stoddard started to shake his finger at the president and said, 'I forbid to you to allow that man on campus,'" Freeman recalled, "I said, 'you can't do that, Bob. We'd be the laughingstock of education. It would be terribly embarrassing and it's wrong. Educational institutions are for disclosure and not for hiding.' He demanded a vote. And I won."

At dinner that night, Freeman and his wife walked into the bar area where Stoddard sat with his "cohorts." The group walked over to Freeman and Stoddard said, "loud enough for everyone to hear, 'Howard, you won fair and square. I want to stay friends.'" And that night, Freeman continued, "the power of the conservatives on the Board dissipated, and they didn't interfere with anything at WPI after that."

As it turned out, Abbie Hoffman declined the WPI invitation; he spoke at Clark University instead. But the revised sentiment among the board members clearly affected Bill Grogan's case for a new approach to education, Freeman said. "All of a sudden, the environment changed to something he could live with, and then things started to move."

The vote on the Plan was a serious matter for every faculty member on campus. "It was a real risk we were taking," said Steve Weininger, a member of the President's Planning Group that framed the initial process to develop the Plan. As an institution, "we could be dead in the water."

Despite the growing need to make WPI stand out from its competitors, resistance among the faculty continued. Bill may have won the battle in 1967, but by the spring of 1970 the stakes were higher and many of his colleagues had seen enough change on campus. He had to work tirelessly to secure every vote.

The lobbying process demanded ingenuity. "A self-described Irish politician at heart, Bill came to the conclusion that, again, the vote was going to be very, very close," Vaz said. He went from department to department, finding supporters who could persuade their colleagues that this was WPI's chance to set itself apart, to offer a unique model for educating future engineers.

But May 1970 was the month of national student strikes, sit-ins, and boycotts. The United States had bombed Cambodia, the National Guard had killed four students at Kent State in Ohio, and front-page debates were about academic freedom and student rights first, curricular change second. It was hard to stay focused on these local issues, no matter how momentous they would be for WPI and its future.

After a flurry of meetings and amendments, the faculty received the news of the final ballot count on May 29, 1970. The tally of written ballots was 92 to 46, with three abstentions, providing precisely the two-to-one margin Bill and the faculty planning committee had hoped for. To persist, wholesale curricular change like the Plan would need overwhelming support.

The Plan had passed and the WPI community was changed forever, but not in every way. After word of the vote had spread, an impromptu victory party ended up at Putnam & Thurston's restaurant in downtown Worcester. On his way there, Bill Grogan stopped by the Phi Kappa Theta fraternity house. Out of the small WPI community he considered his extended family, Bill wanted one particular student committee member to come join him in the victory celebration.

Ron Zarrella '71 was honored, but protested to his faculty advisor that it was the night before his electromagnetic theory exam, and the junior had a lot of studying left to do.

"You're a smart kid," Bill told him. "If you don't know it now, you won't learn it in two hours." Besides, Zarrella's professor, Willy Eggimann, was waiting in the car. The evening included much singing and many speeches.

"I passed, got a C in the course," Zarrella said with a smile. "Of course, it didn't help my GPA." But he had been given the chance to witness a sea change in undergraduate education. In the long run, he would find that going along for a ride with Bill Grogan could be one of the best decisions he'd ever make.

CHAPTER TWO

To Make Our Good College an Excellent One

What can undergraduates do?
Just about whatever is expected of them.
—Bill Grogan

WHEN BILL GROGAN completed his wartime service with the Navy, he knew he needed to learn more and WPI was where he wanted to be. The work he had done in electronics for the U.S. Naval Electronics Laboratory while aboard the USS *Marysville* in California helped confirm for him what the next step on his educational path should be. He enrolled in WPI's master's program for electrical engineering, returning to campus in the fall of 1946, just over a year after he'd left.

"In addition to obtaining valuable knowledge," WPI's course catalog explained, "the character of graduate work is such that the student will develop self-reliance, power of independent action, and ability to apply scientific methods to engineering problems. The graduate student is given considerable freedom in selecting his courses. Definite schedules are not prescribed, because it is felt that the elective system, with its opportunity for specializations, offers decided advantages in graduate work."

Above: *Eager to innovate in the classroom, Grogan was dismayed by WPI's rigidity.*

9

Undergraduates were not so lucky. In most four-year programs, they had only two electives. Classes ran through Saturday morning, and by the early 1950s they were followed by mandatory ROTC drills for freshmen and sophomores.

For his graduate degree, Bill needed only to choose 36 semester hours of courses. He took a summer course at MIT in electrical engineering to work toward a June 1949 graduation. His studies led him to develop his master's thesis on the development of a high-voltage laboratory, working with WPI classmate and graduate assistant Norman Padden '46, '50 (MS EE) during the spring of 1949.

As part of his research, Bill ran the EE department's high-voltage electrostatic spark generator. The 1907 department building, Atwater Kent Laboratories, was the first in the nation specifically designed for electrical engineering. Built in the shape of a capital E, its design included an enormous bay, once used as an electric trolley car testing plant. Though the test car had been dismantled in 1927, the trolley bay-turned-laboratory retained a traveling overhead crane to maneuver heavy equipment, and housed the high-voltage generator. A balcony ringed the cavernous space.

Here Bill hosted what came to be known as "spark parties," attended by as many as 50 students and their dates on Saturday evenings. As John Burgarella '50 recalled, the couples would gather on the balcony to watch "a display of lightning bolts from the high-voltage generator, operated by Bill." The show got even better, Burgarella said, after Bill took a log with a nail hammered into it, wrapped it with wire, and then blew it apart with a jolt of electricity.

Upon receiving his master of science degree at Commencement in June 1949, Bill was named an assistant professor in the Electrical Engineering Department, one of the Institute's six degree-granting departments. There he joined four other assistant professors, six professors, a professor emeritus, three instructors, two graduate assistants, a lab assistant, and a shop assistant.

During World War II, the department had conformed to the Navy's program to educate the hundreds of officer candidates arriving on campus as part of the V-12 program. "The impact of the V-12 years on WPI's curricula was dramatic," Bill recalled. "The sudden infusion of electronics as a very high Navy priority for the EE curriculum really changed the culture of the department." WPI's focus had been on power, but the new focus allowed electronics professor Hobart Newell, "with the help of some physics faculty, to lead WPI and its fortunate graduates into the rapidly emerging world of electronics."

In 1949 the academic year was divided into two terms, each 17 weeks long with a week of final examinations. Summer shop was an additional requirement, held in June or September, depending on the student's major department. At the time, the student headcount was just over 800, including a handful of "post-graduate" students. Major decisions for the school's administration were made by the president, the dean of the faculty, and the Executive Committee of the faculty, which consisted of the dean of the faculty and the four engineering department heads. Monthly faculty meetings in Alden Memorial primarily involved news announcements. No one spoke, except the president and the dean.

Bill taught several introductory EE courses and a course on alternating current circuits, typically taken by juniors. Burgarella, who had continued into WPI's graduate program, was happy to work with Bill as his graduate teaching assistant in the AC circuits class. Some days he provided more assistance than others.

"Bill was teaching the students how to do calculations in AC circuits one day," Burgarella recalled. "They're different from calculating direct current circuits," and they involve complex numbers, which can't be divided. "There's a trick to doing it." As Bill started to explain the trick, his mind went blank. Not missing a beat, he told the class, "and now Mr. Burgarella will show you how to divide by a complex number."

"He was businesslike but fun," Burgarella said. "I always looked up to him."

Though his teaching career was interrupted in 1951 when he was re-called to Navy service, Bill quickly won the admiration of his students. He was tapped for WPI's senior honorary society, Skull, at a special dinner held in his honor at his fraternity, Theta Kappa Phi, just days before his deployment. He was the thirteenth member of the faculty or administration to join the august group: "… those whose efforts in the best interest of Tech merit especial honor," noted the student newspaper, *Tech News*.

"Prof. Grogan will long be remembered by those undergraduates with whom he has had contact as an excellent teacher, thorough and conscientious, with a flair for clear and simple presentation," the article continued. "He has always had a deep interest in the future of the Institute, which he has recently served in a public relations capacity, and in the future of individual students, to whom he has often been a counselor."

Advisor and Academic Life Guide

Advising students was Bill Grogan's most enduring passion. While still in graduate school, he was faculty advisor to his fraternity. In his first two years as a faculty member, he served as advisor to the journalism honor society, Pi Delta Epsilon, returning after his military leave to be the group's advisor for another eight years. He became the faculty advisor for Tau Beta Pi, a national engineering fraternity of students of "distinguished scholarship and exemplary character."

That year was also the first of fourteen he would serve as counselor to the WPI student branch of the American Institute of Electrical Engineers (AIEE) and the Institute of Radio Engineers (IRE), groups that later merged to form the Institute of Electrical and Electronics Engineers (IEEE). As those merger plans got under way, he joined the branch merger committee and later the student branches committee. He chaired an ad hoc committee on student branch criteria, and the district student activities committee. In 1966 he served as regional director of student activities for IEEE.

Involvement with these professional organizations helped his EE students establish their first academic credentials. WPI hosted the first all-student IRE convention in 1952 and the city of Worcester served as occasional host for AIEE district student conventions. At both organizations' regional competitions, WPI students regularly presented prize-winning papers.

Bill's service on student-related faculty committees began in 1954, after his return from military service, first with the Scholarships Committee and then, from 1955 to 1971, on the Freshmen Advisory Committee. While he spent much time overhauling WPI's overall academic offerings in many ways, Bill continued to focus on the challenges of the freshman year and the importance of advising in that critical transition from high school to college expectations.

When he was later named dean of undergraduate studies, Bill remained an academic advisor for a few students every year, a connection he valued as a source of insights on student interests and concerns. Or as he noted, "Advising helps close the feedback loop on an otherwise open education system." It was a role he reluctantly concluded only in 2008. That May, he wrote to his former advisee, friend, and fraternity brother Pete Miraglia '95 that the Commencement ceremony would mark the graduation of the final advisee of his career. "I have had academic advisees since 1947—61 years! Even during my 20 years as dean I always kept advisees—partly because it kept me in stimulating contact with the students for whom the whole show is really all about, and partly because it gave me a sense of what was really happening— independent of what I was being fed through the 'system.'"

He took the role seriously, and encouraged other faculty members to follow his example. WPI hosted an advising conference in 2000, and although already 10 years into his retirement, Bill gladly offered his substantive and colorfully expressed thoughts on what he saw as not just an obligation but a calling for his colleagues.

"Without interaction with an experienced faculty member, students are on their own to wade through unfocused resources," he said. "They often drift through their academic careers like dead fish floating with the tides."

It is the advisor's role, he would say, to help give students a sense of direction "I am often reminded of my days in the Navy when we would look down from the bridge and see the sailors shining the brass, adjusting the radars, and calibrating the guns, yet most of them had little idea of where the ship was going."

Faculty members need to connect with their advisees at every stage of their academic experience, he urged, but particularly in the freshman year. He recommended taking students to lunch, describing the inexpensive sandwiches at the Northworks restaurant near campus as "a great investment on $20,000 tuition." Students who shared details about "their families, their dogs, and their hopes in life" were more likely to seek advice when facing challenges both academic and personal. Bill would even attend financial aid meetings with his advisees, and arrange for tutorials if they needed to make up credits.

Defining advising as a "core academic responsibility where the *entire* education process is integrated," he concluded that advising is nothing less than where "students who come to WPI trusting us with their intellectual lives are helped to achieve their full potential as human beings."

EARLY RUMBLINGS

Bill returned to campus from his tour of duty with the Navy with a renewed energy for teaching. He was assigned several introductory EE courses that were intended for sophomores. Mastering those fundamental skills laid the foundation for their later success as electrical engineers, but in his opinion, the presentation of the material was less than engaging. In his classrooms, he wanted to try another approach.

He didn't waste much time, and it seemed his timing was good. His department head, Theodore Morgan, was nearing the end of his career at WPI, having served in that role since 1931 with three years absence for military service during World War II. Morgan demonstrated for Bill the planning process, a long-held strength of the Institute and an established part of school culture, applied (at least) for small-scale challenges.

Years later, EE professor Bill Roadstrum explained this process to a group of new faculty:

> First, one states the objectives of his planning. Second, outline the present situation or difficulties as they pertain to that objective.

Third, list the possible directions that could be pursued to obtain the objective. Fourth, analyze each of these possible directions in itself and against the others. Fifth, select the best objective. Last, you have to tie the whole decision together with the necessary detail, and this is usually described as making the logistics work out.

As Bill resumed teaching in the spring semester of 1953, Morgan had released a department study of its educational effectiveness using various student success measures. The study found that students had little exposure to electrical engineering prior to their selection of an EE major, their study habits were not as serious as the returning veterans in earlier class years, and graduates were heading increasingly to just a few large companies to begin their careers.

"Our present students probably compare well with their predecessors in native ability," the report began, "but a great deal more salesmanship and a higher standard of instruction is required to develop and maintain their interest." Reviewing some of the goals of EE faculty instruction, the report noted that students should sharpen their ability to think and reason, develop resourcefulness and initiative, and "inculcate certain required technical information."

Bill's idea was to develop resourcefulness and initiative among the sophomores as they were first exposed to the field of electrical engineering while learning that technical information. Taking a page from the junior and senior year curriculum (the stage when students first witnessed any practical applications of the field's fundamental knowledge), he asked sophomores to take what they had previously learned in basic math and science courses and bring in the new material in electrical circuit theory to understand how interrelated systems worked together.

He changed the two-course series from "Electric and Magnetic Principles" to "Fundamentals of Electrical Engineering" and expected the sophomores to begin their transformation into competent engineers from the first week of classes. Feedback from students was extremely positive and Bill continued to revisit the EE curriculum whenever possible.

One of the first sophomores to take his reconstituted course was

Bradley McKenzie '58, who later reflected that he had "yet to find a better qualified teacher in every aspect of the word than Professor Grogan. He has a rare combination of professional competence and personal magnetism."

Off campus, Bill was recognized for his early interest in educational change. In 1954 he participated in a "Veritas Forum," where the president of Holy Cross spoke on "A Liberal Arts Education: Is It Worth It?" Panel members, including Bill and representatives from Becker Junior College and the Massachusetts Department of Education, then examined the question from several angles.

EXAMINING STUDENT MOTIVATION

In December 1956 Bill joined a short-term faculty committee with the comprehensive name Committee on Student Scholarship, Motivation, and Morale. Joseph Zimmerman, an associate professor of economics, government, and business, chaired the committee, which was formed shortly after he published a brief article in the *WPI Journal* describing a study of student motivation.

"Formal education is an organized and guided quest for knowledge," Zimmerman wrote. "Unfortunately not all college students are actively and energetically engaged in this quest." Which motives spur students to work, he asked, and which discourage them from working?

Bill was one of ten committee members, and he joined a subcommittee examining the grading system, together with Richard Morton, associate professor of physics, and Ernest Hollows, assistant dean of students and admissions.

After surveying grade distributions at peer institutions and across departments and class years at WPI, the subcommittee noted in a preliminary report that few professors ever submitted a grade over 90 and students had too many chances to retake exams as "conditions" if their grade was between 45 and 60. Freshman grading should be less stringent as attempts to "shake up" the new students proved demoralizing. Not surprisingly, low grades correlated with lack of study. The final subcommittee report, submitted in November 1957, had no mention of freshman grading, but recommended changes in passing, conditioning, and failing grades. It also established a system of probation and a requirement that students achieve a minimum weighted average of 65 or better to qualify for a degree.

There clearly was room for change in other aspects of WPI's educational ecosystem. Beyond grading, subcommittees studied the school's facilities, extracurricular activities, fraternities, student-faculty relations, and contact hours, relative to peer institutions. Internal reports noted the need for a central library, greater on-campus medical care, fewer roommates per dormitory room, after-class access to classrooms for group study (with careful consideration of the additional heating costs), faculty attendance at student functions, athletic events and fraternity dinners, clearer explanations of course expectations from faculty, posted office hours, and limited negative remarks to students when returning papers with low grades.

The May 1958 final summary report, signed by Dean Lawrence "Cookie" Price, pointed out (somewhat belatedly) that many other faculty committees were concerned with similar topics and the subcommittees stood ready to share their systematic findings with those existing groups. There appears to have been little immediate change in response to the report, and the committee disbanded.

Change remained possible within the EE department, however, and Bill continued to revise courses as he could. In 1958 the senior-level Engineering Economy course description changed significantly from "principles of economics" to "the impact economic factors could have on engineering projects." With enrollment capped at 25 or 30 seniors, Bill's course had a waitlist every year.

During his first class, he would read Oxford scholar Sir Richard Livingstone's definition of an engineering technician: "a man who understands everything about his job—except its ultimate purpose and its place in the order of the universe." He then told the gathered seniors, "It is the aim of this class to, in part, help overcome this problem." One of the assigned readings was William H. Whyte's 1956 bestselling book *The Organization Man,* now a classic, which examined the social structures and assumptions of corporate America.

"He would bring up a topic and ask the classroom, 'what do you guys think?'" recalled Jack Bresnahan '68. "Engineering economics was a step toward management." Groups of three to five students were assigned projects with local companies. Their challenges drew on everything they had learned, and a lot of what they didn't know, too.

Bresnahan's project at Norton Company involved developing a new way to measure the grade of the company's grinding wheel, updating a methodology that had been in use for a hundred years. His midterm was a presentation on the proposal to a group of factory foremen. A mechanical engineering major, Bresnahan said his project group included four electrical engineers. They described their idea "talking at the PhD level," he said, which did not go over well with the foremen. So they simplified the presentation for their final exam, which, of course, included several PhD degree holders "and three vice presidents," he said, laughing. He went on to a successful career with Norton (which is today a division of Saint-Gobain) after fulfilling his military service with the Navy. He also ensured that Norton hosted many more student projects.

"Bill didn't get enough credit as a teacher," said Ron Zarrella '71, who also took Bill's Engineering Economics course. His project team worked with early computing advances at Wright Computers. Their task was to design a 96-column punch card that would run faster and do more than the existing 36-column cards. "We completed it and we're all on the patent as contributors," he said.

But the lessons he learned involved far more than punch cards. "The important thing about these projects is they went way beyond the technology," he said. "We had to answer questions like, 'What do we do with this product? Who wants it? Who will pay for it? And there were more esoteric questions like, 'What is the economic value provided versus what is available today?'

"Our product was all about speed," Zarrella said, "and then IBM blew right past us" with a much faster card reader, rendering their invention obsolete. While painful, he said, "that was a valuable lesson."

SEVEN YEARS AFTER SPUTNIK

In 1964, as advances in technology sped along while the United States focused on a space race with the Soviet Union, few of those developments were visible on the WPI campus. "Seven years after Sputnik," Bill said many times, "the American science and engineering community had been shocked into action. Nowhere was the shock greater than in the American universities." Millions of government dollars poured into campuses to upgrade science and engineering programs. Yet at WPI, little had changed. Courses were taught as they always had been.

President Harry Storke had arrived on campus in 1962 after retiring from a successful Army career as a lieutenant general, most recently as commander of NATO's land forces in southeastern Europe. By 1963 he had outlined a long-range plan for new buildings and facilities, including a central library. Bill recalled how the new president had called WPI "an undiscovered educational gem." In keeping with his military training, however, President Storke respected the existing hierarchy and looked to the Executive Committee of the faculty to create its own long-range plan for education at WPI. He urged the department heads to rethink what the school had to offer.

In late 1963 he hosted a two-day academic planning retreat at Old Sturbridge Village. As Bill would later write about the event, "At the conclusion of the first day, the participants politely concluded that the curriculum was just about as fine as it could be. Before breakfast the next morning, the very frustrated president asked Dean Price to tell the participants that, after finishing their breakfasts, they should return to their offices. The retreat was over."

"We had a pretty traditional program at the school," Professor Romeo Moruzzi recounted to a group of new faculty members in 1976. "It was rigid, lock-step, very little flexibility, almost no experimentation going on. The students were pretty much being smothered under a whole selection of required courses. The professor felt that he had his textbook and he had a blackboard, and you didn't need much else. It was quite a straight-laced environment."

A group of EE professors was ready to loosen those laces. Starting in the late 1950s, they'd been meeting informally on Friday afternoons at Bigelow's Tavern in downtown Worcester, floating new ideas in the city's oldest pub.

"At WPI, there was not a faculty club, as such," said Bill. But faculty members still wanted a place to gather and talk. "Over a period of time," he continued, "a group of young professors from several departments would meet at Bigelow's to have a few beers and discuss WPI, their departments, and the world."

A constant refrain, Bill said later, was that "the curriculum didn't allow for experimentation to the degree we wanted. We wanted freedom in developing new courses, new approaches to things. And we talked about them, and how we did it." Bill could point to the shifts he had made in his EE courses, or as he said, "how we snuck in things that we could do to bring this about."

Faculty in the EE department knew that their department head's first word was always "no." "He wouldn't buy a three-hole punch" when one punch would do, said Willy Eggimann, who had joined the department in 1964. "That was the beginning."

By early 1965, however, they wanted to shift from generalized gripe sessions to taking actual steps, so they formed a study group. Professors from other departments joined them, and the group at Bigelow's Tavern grew to as many as 15 or 20 people, Bill said later.

In mid-March 1965, the group produced a report outlining their initial thoughts about the undergraduate curriculum, both within the EE department and more broadly at WPI. A year later, they prepared a progress report on their initial findings and asked EE department head Glen Richardson to bring it to the Executive Committee, the people who held the power to enact change at WPI.

"Our department head at the time was not particularly interested in bringing this forth," Moruzzi told the new faculty members. But fate, and professional development, intervened. "We had a long-standing tradition in the Electrical Engineering Department of going to the IEEE convention in New York, arranging a table one night at a hofbrau house, and asking our former students to join us there." As it turned out, Richardson sat between Moruzzi and Grogan.

"After about a half-gallon of good German beer," Moruzzi recounted, "we proceeded to tell him that either he got the report out or we would." And so on March 30, 1966, Richardson sent Bill Grogan in his place to the Executive Committee, where Bill introduced the memorandum the group had prepared.

POLISHING THE GEM

The opening section of Bill's presentation included ideas that may have seemed heretical at the time:

> It is the responsibility of the faculty to actively participate in establishing academic goals for its college and to seek out methods by which these goals may be achieved. ... A periodic review of the overall operation of the academic curriculum as a whole is thus a necessity. The formulation of a long-range academic goal requires a broad survey of the entire engineering curriculum.

President Storke attended that meeting, and in Moruzzi's opinion, "this was the first time it dawned on him that the faculty might be concerned in this area or have something to say."

Going through the official channels, the president asked Dean Price for a report from the EE department. The following week, on April 6, 1966, Richardson presented to the Executive Committee the study group's "proposal for freshman curriculum and general considerations regarding the entire curriculum."

The document began, "... to say that our freshman students have been having some difficulties is an understatement," and suggested that "the freshman year is a transition period for all students, and we of the faculty, with our broader perspective and experience, should use this to the fullest to help aid the freshman in his metamorphosis from a high school student to a participating member of an intellectual community." It followed with more background information and a detailed program for freshmen.

Bill said the presentation to the committee was "like throwing an anvil into a room full of feathers. You didn't even hear the thud."

From that silence arose the Curriculum Study Committee.

FIRST CRACKS APPEAR IN THE OLD ORDER

As the new academic year approached, it became clear that no response to any proposals would be forthcoming from the Executive Committee. It seemed paralyzed in the face of what Dean Price had termed "the race to keep pace with ceaseless change" in an April 1966 *WPI Journal* article describing the incremental modifications that WPI's curriculum had undergone since 1959.

By late summer 1966 President Storke and Dean Price were ready for action. Together, they made a call to Bill Grogan. Would he accept their request to chair WPI's first all-faculty curriculum committee? The assignment would be to focus on the freshman and sophomore years. Bill told them he needed a week to respond.

The call had come at a pivotal moment in his life. He had just married Mae Jeanne Kafer, a young widow from Manhattan. After years of consulting for the Navy, Bill had received an attractive job offer from the Department of the Navy. The offer was appealing on two fronts. First, it was an important position that promised to make full use of Bill's engineering skills. Second, it would mean moving to Washington, D.C., and Bill knew Mae would be happier living in such a cosmopolitan city than in Worcester. "Although I loved teaching, WPI, and the academic life," Bill reflected later, "I had become increasingly discouraged by the apparent continued resistance to change and my growing lack of hope for the future at WPI."

Still, the new committee would offer Bill a way "to participate in real change," he wrote. While acknowledging that the position in Washington "would be lucrative and exciting," he concluded that "when it was all over, my efforts really wouldn't make much of a difference."

It was a long week for Bill, marked by lengthy conversations with Mae and a great deal of soul-searching. In the end, energized by the new committee's possibilities, he made the choice to remain at the Institute. "I knew I had coupled my future to that of WPI's," he reflected.

Each academic department nominated three candidates for the committee, and President Storke made the final selections. The committee's 10 members included independent-minded faculty from across the disciplines, including economics, English, and physical education. They were prepared to challenge some long-held traditions.

The curriculum had the opportunity to address an emerging professional deficit. In the workplace, "we found that engineers had become known as automatons," said Bill. "They were good at mechanically solving problems, but didn't understand what the effect was on society and on people."

The first of the committee's two reports, submitted in February 1967, noted that the majority of committee members shared the opinions voiced in a September 1966 report published by the Panel on Engineering Education convened by the Engineers Joint Council for Professional Development as part of its call for a total reassessment of engineering education:

> To prepare engineering students for rapid technological change and for growing responsibilities in industry and government, the emphasis in instruction must be placed more upon the development of the potential capabilities and insights of the individual, and less upon the transfer of generally prescribed contents in standardized courses.

The members of the Curriculum Study Committee let this national report from a respected professional organization speak for them and put their advocacy for change in a broader context:

> It is how the teacher uses knowledge and wisdom in the student that counts, not the facts a student knows at some precise time. ... The educational process must be adjusted to the student and not the student to the process. ... It would be most unfortunate if a vested interest in what the individual teacher knows of past accumulated knowledge were to continue to be the major focus of teaching. ... The teacher of engineering today must prepare students for a profession

facing rapid change. He must create a want for discovery and not be satisfied with a competent transfer of past knowledge and known techniques.

What that preparation would mean for instruction at WPI was a complete overhaul of the freshman and sophomore academic program, an increase in the number of elective courses, the introduction of new minors, and the development of an academic advisory system.

The Curriculum Study Committee's report echoed Sir Richard Livingstone's warning about engineering technicians and reflected glimmers of findings from the short-lived Student Scholarship, Motivation, and Morale Committee with its focus on the freshman year experience and the importance of advising. Work that had occurred in faculty committees years earlier but had never been enacted was finally coming to light. The committee embraced ideas stemming from department discussions held across campus (and in Bigelow's Tavern), not just from electrical engineering.

Included in this first report were specific proposals for a new freshman-sophomore curriculum, including a lighter course load for freshmen, a one-credit first-semester course on "digital computers as a problem-solving tool," and a transition schedule for minors in the humanities. The report called for a pilot phase involving half the freshmen class for the coming 1967–68 academic year.

It also included a minority report, penned by mechanical engineering professor Leighton Wellman, a member of the faculty since 1930, long-standing supporter of the drawing requirement for all freshmen, and author of the definitive textbook on the subject. He spoke for those students who looked to WPI to provide an engineering education, with any additional time focused on those ever-expanding scientific and technological topics, rather than in the humanities and social sciences.

"The value of these courses to the scientist or engineer in achieving his career objectives has long been promoted, conceded by many, but never actually confirmed by any scientific or statistical methods," Wellman asserted.

He also argued for retention of two required freshman courses that offered an overview of science and engineering fields, and more important, gave students "an appreciation of real-life engineering problems and situations." He continued, "It is not enough to lecture about engineering; the freshman needs to experience it." He would find much support for this position in a few short years.

The Executive Committee forwarded this first report to the broader faculty for a vote on April 20, 1967. The new freshman-sophomore curricular proposal was approved overwhelmingly, as was the minors program. Even more significantly, the faculty as a whole had made a decision to change direction within the school's academic structure.

The second Curriculum Study Committee report, released on May 2, 1967, asked for the adoption of new degree programs in economics, business management, and humanities and technology.

Recognizing the school's tight finances, however, it was quick to note the limited impact these programs would have on the finances of the institution, stating on its opening page, "The programs recommended herein, heavily dependent upon the Minors Programs established in Report #1, may be implemented without an increase in the size of our present faculty and no courses are proposed in this report for which we do not have an existing faculty capability."

The proposal detailed two- and three-year course sequences for the new majors. The committee also asked the faculty to vote on their proposal for a bachelor of science degree without a specified major to accommodate interdisciplinary interests among students headed into medicine, architecture, or other professions that lacked a specified pre-professional track. Wellman signed the report, but resigned from the committee shortly thereafter.

On May 18, 1967, the faculty voted to accept the Curriculum Study Committee's second report in its entirety. There was much more to be done, as Bill Grogan told the student newspaper, but the new library, which had just opened, would greatly help with the establishment of these new programs. Looking back on this vote later, he explained that the more important long-range accomplishment of this committee was "the demonstration that change was indeed possible at WPI." Change notably orchestrated by an empowered faculty.

While the Curriculum Study Committee cemented these historic and far-reaching changes, its chairman made the headlines. The same issue of *Tech News* that reported on the new degree programs named Bill Grogan "WPI Man of the Year," praising the "outstanding achievement and exemplary display of character" in his work as committee chair, and recognizing the "voluminous amount of work necessary for the success of this project."

The *Tech News* recognition hinted at an asset that would be integral to Bill's success throughout his career: his boundless energy. "I've never met anyone so action-oriented and able to tap into so much inner energy," Pete Miraglia said. "He was a ball of fire. That made him a force multiplier, able to do all that exhausting, relentless legwork, politicking, debating, and so on late into the night, every day. I'm sure this must have inspired the people around him."

Grogan noted that the committee had raised numerous other topics, which remained for further discussion, that were as wide-ranging as those in its two reports. They included advanced placement, junior college transfers, four- to five-year BS/MS programs, an honors program, a quarter system, a biology or pre-med program, an undergraduate research program, more languages, coordination with other colleges, pass/fail grades, ROTC, physical education, and more pre-professional courses.

What Kind of School Will We Have?

The ripples of these new ideas spread beyond WPI's immediate campus community. A few months after the historic faculty vote, an article appeared in the *WPI Journal*, penned by Charles Feldman, an MIT alumnus who had come to WPI from Northeastern in 1965 to teach mechanical engineering. His title: "Whither Worcester Tech?"

Applying the engineering problem-solving approach to the Institute, Feldman defined the problem and identified the constraints to a solution.

He noted the threat that growing state universities posed to private universities such as WPI. To compete with them, and justify charging far higher tuition rates, WPI would have to provide "the BEST science and engineering education in the country—not a good education or a quality education—but an education that is truly unique."

Feldman's attitude and some of the language of his article drew heavily on the Curriculum Study Committee report. He broached the then-radical ideas of adopting individual and small-group learning styles, examining human values, and encouraging students to take responsibility for their own education. The stakes were high, not just for WPI's survival but for the nation's technological edge.

He concluded his article by asking, "Do we dare aspire to greatness?"

The answer from President Storke was an emphatic "yes," but it was an answer painfully slow in coming. Once more, he asked the Executive Committee of the faculty for a long-range educational plan for the school. Their response was not as far-reaching as he had hoped. Thus, more than a year after the publication of Feldman's article, Storke shocked the senior administrative team when he announced his appointment of a president's planning group (PPG) in December 1968.

Their mandate: Present creative, broad new objectives for the Institute and establish the principles upon which a renewed, modern mission could be established. And report back quickly, as he was planning to retire at the end of June 1969.

In the nineteen months between the Curriculum Study Committee vote and President Storke's PPG announcement, the faculty had not stood still. The WPI chapter of the American Association of University Professors (AAUP) had been activated in 1964, and in late November 1967 it hosted an open meeting on the issues of tenure and academic freedom. Two subcommittees formed to examine two sides of the issue: how tenure could be granted at WPI, and how tenured faculty might be removed.

In April 1968, breaking all protocol during a faculty meeting, a faculty committee was proposed and elected to prepare a tenure policy. Within a month, it had submitted its report, and its recommendations were approved unanimously by faculty vote. On June 14, 1968, WPI's trustees voted to adopt the tenure policy, effective July 1. At the September 1968 faculty meeting, the first faculty tenure committee was elected.

As the curricular structure began to shift at WPI, so did the governance structure. In June 1970 the trustees voted to adopt the constitution that WPI faculty had proposed in April 1969 and approved in March 1970. The formerly all-powerful Executive Committee was redefined as an administrative committee of the faculty. Institutional decision making now included far more faculty members than ever before in school history. "The timely establishment of WPI's new faculty governance system," wrote Bill, "proved an extremely important factor in the later successful implementation of the WPI Plan."

President Storke had selected carefully the leadership of the President's Planning Group. He asked former World War II Marine and chemical engineering professor Bill Shipman to lead the effort. Even before Feldman's article on Tech's future, Shipman had authored a thoughtful piece, "Two Pressures on Tech," in the March-April 1966 *WPI Journal*, projecting the impact of a growing research enterprise together with expanding course offerings, and suggesting as the ultimate solution a program designed to teach the student to learn. For the PPG, Shipman should include EE professor Bill Roadstrum, Storke requested, but was free to name the rest. The new group chair asked John van Alstyne from Mathematics, Charles Heventhal from English, Steve Weininger from Chemistry, and Jack Boyd from Mechanical Engineering to join the team.

Grogan later noted that he and Moruzzi had both been considered, but he was occupied implementing curricular changes as chairman of the new Freshman-Sophomore Curricula Planning Committee and serving on the search committee for Storke's successor. For his part, Moruzzi was focused on "WPI's new faculty-inspired, complex drive to organize and implement a totally new faculty governance system," Bill recalled. Both participated in informal discussions with the new group.

"There was some ferment going on," Moruzzi said later, "not only on the academic side but on the governance side, and it started to really crystallize. ... All the action took place in the space of two years, 1968–70. It was conducted by various faculty members, with no time off from all their other duties."

While the PPG mandate was clear, President Storke put no restrictions on the group's work, telling them "take this wherever it leads you." The project parameters expanded beyond even the president's vision. Roadstrum felt that "the problems that the planning committee addressed at that time at WPI are really the eternal problems of engineering education."

DO WE DARE ASPIRE TO GREATNESS?

Full of positive energy, and somewhat amazed that the president was encouraging wholesale changes, the PPG solicited ideas from all quarters and vowed from the start that all suggestions would be treated seriously, no matter how outlandish. One committee member wrote a cautionary essay early in the process that warned, "It is almost impossible for our proposals to be extreme. It is, however, very likely that they will be too routine."

Within the first month, Bill shared his thoughts with the PPG, concerned that WPI, blind to its own potential as an educational innovator, might sell itself short. Was there enough belief in the Institute by students and faculty to really do anything like this, he wondered?

> I most sincerely believe the college should develop its identity as a student-oriented educational institution of merit. In the process, it should become a small technological university, changing its name if that should be necessary, to reflect its development. We must recognize that the changing world around us requires that all our graduates realize that after all on this planet, it is the people who really count, not just their machines. We are paying a price for the sterility of engineering and science education in the past. We must have enough faith in the future of Worcester Tech to really believe that this college can overcome old inferiority complexes and dare to create, innovate, and lead the educational world into a new concept of adjusting machine markers to people.

29

The PPG worked tirelessly to pull together its first report, "A Planning Program for Worcester Polytechnic Institute: The Future of Two Towers," which came to be known as "Two Towers I." The March 1969 report was extensive, thoughtful, and thought-provoking—and well received by the faculty.

It featured an integration of wide-ranging research on the state of higher education in the country, both in engineering and the liberal arts, and examined the new position of the engineer in the world:

> If one accepts the concept of today's engineer as "the mediator between knowledge and society" (*Critique of a College*, Swarthmore College, November 1967), then the role of the engineer should be an increasingly vital and exciting one in our culture. He should be the "competent generalist," the "problem solver," the "decision maker" within a broader spectrum of his environment than in the past. He must accept as part of his task the definition of the consequences of technological advances. That is, he must understand the ecology of man.

Taking an unflinching look at WPI's current situation as well as a broader view of the potential the institution held to confront the world's mounting challenges, the hard-working PPG members had spoken with faculty and students, and assessed the school's perception among alumni, community members, peer institutions, industry, and society at large. Each of these constituencies would exert some degree of influence on the long-term feasibility of achieving selected goals.

In the group's analysis of the school, their report began concisely, "Worcester Polytechnic Institute is a small, private, traditional engineering and science college. All of these adjectives are important." It looked to its history to help frame a new vision and purpose:

> Tech's original double concept [the balance of theory and practice] was seen then as remedying a common fault—the irrelevance of collegiate education to most everyday professional pursuits—particularly for the growing technical and mechanical fields.

> Could this same problem be the unifying theme between the 1870s

and 1970s? Is the Two Towers concept still that of making "theoretic knowledge" relevant to the student by "practical training" in its application to today's problems?"

"Two Towers I" proffered a list of twelve possible objectives for the school and a set of criteria to evaluate those objectives. It began an evaluation process for four of the objectives, with others to be evaluated in the next report, due out in June 1969. A third report would be expected in September, and a final one the following March, for action by the faculty before June 30, 1970.

Recognizing the urgency of the timeframe and a natural tendency for groups to resist taking final action, the initial "Two Towers" report cautioned, "Unless some schedule closely approximating that proposed is adopted, WPI's time as a private operation is limited. Obviously, the number of people involved with planning will have to be increased markedly to insure the success of the proposed schedule."

"We really did go about this in a very systematic way with a pretty good grasp of the planning process," recounted Roadstrum in his 1976 presentation to new faculty. But this level of long-term strategic planning was beyond any previous efforts known to the planning group. The trustees had developed ten-year plans, but those had not been shared widely. In effect, the report was asking, "what are the problems and what are the solutions?"

The student newspaper reported mixed reactions to the ground-breaking report. Although many students were preparing to leave for spring vacation, those who had read it had responses "varying from wildly enthusiastic to a somewhat cynical view." Faculty views, as Bill Grogan related to the reporter, were a "mixture of apprehension (when confronted with cold reality) with expectation of an opportunity to make Tech a really exciting institution."

Grogan found that the document "did not produce startling informa-tion" as it analyzed the current, known situation for WPI, but "it pro-vides a jumping-off point for something we've never done before—that is, to determine where we're going. Nobody saw the problems in their entirety. … It's the most significant document I've seen in many years."

To seek greater input on ten of the twelve possible objectives (excluding "to maintain the status quo" and an "appropriate combination of the above"), to hear new ideas, and to persuade students that the faculty really was serious about listening to their opinions, the PPG held a campuswide planning day on Wednesday, April 16, 1969.

As Weininger later explained, it was a historic day in many ways, but particularly because it was the first time WPI had ever cancelled classes. "To appreciate that, you have to realize WPI had a history and a Calvinistic pride in the fact that it had never cancelled classes since it opened in 1865," he said. "Neither rain nor sleet, earthquakes, nor the infirmities of the faculty had ever resulted in the closing of the doors."

SEIZE THE DAY

Anticipating the day off, one columnist for *Tech News* urged student participation and supported greater faculty voices in the school's decision making. Addressing the faculty, he wrote, "Gentlemen, Worcester Tech is undergoing a revolution. The students are behind you. Carpe Diem!"

About 150 students took part in the discussions, some ten percent of the student body. About 140 faculty members and a smattering of trustees attended as well. Meeting in rooms across the campus, they broke into smaller groups and everyone's voice was heard, no matter who they were. Professors were impressed by how articulate the students were, students saw professors as human "for the first time," and the event was described by a reporter as "the most intellectually stimulating day I've ever experienced." Many asserted that follow-up would be essential.

Concluded one student with some foresight, "It may well be that the origination of this planning effort will be what President Storke is most remembered for at Tech."

The June 1969 report, nicknamed "Two Towers II," summed up the day succinctly. "It would appear that WPI has underestimated the latent hunger for experimentation and intellectual excitement that lies within this college community."

News of the potential sea changes on campus proved attractive for the presidential search prospects. Shortly after the April Planning Day, George Hazzard accepted the search committee's offer to become WPI's eleventh president on July 1, 1969. His memo to the faculty said he was eager to see real plans for action and expected a full report by early September.

Acknowledging the intensive job of document preparation and coordination involved in the next stage of the planning process, President Storke appointed Roy Seaberg, a member of the admissions staff and assistant secretary of the WPI Alumni Association, as the PPG's executive secretary.

With the publication of that second report, the PPG disbanded. As it moved on from an institutional assessment process to generate a plan that would be implemented by the faculty, the committee members felt they needed to be seen as truly representing their faculty peers, and not the president who had appointed them. Their successors were elected by faculty vote on June 3. The committee size remained unchanged, but Bill Roadstrum and Steve Weininger, who chose not to run for election due to the pressure of completing a book, were replaced by Bill Grogan and Romeo Moruzzi. Seaberg stayed on through the summer.

"Bill was a very positive, wonderful addition to the committee, of course," said original PPG member Heventhal. "He enjoyed the atmosphere that we had already created, and he flourished."

"For Bill, this represented the culmination of what he'd been trying to achieve for years," added Weininger. "He threw himself into the work."

OLD SOLUTIONS WON'T SOLVE NEW PROBLEMS

The newly elected committee had a clear summer job description, first outlined in the original Two Towers report, which specified their next deadline as September 1969:

- From the preliminary analyses, select those objectives or combinations of objectives which seem best.

- Set up a structure for detailed analyses of selected objectives and assign chairmen for full development of each.
- Report to policy-making agencies of the school.

It was a very full three months. The committee first focused on a goals statement, which naturally led to a statement of educational philosophy, and then to an outline of how that philosophy would translate into a curriculum, degree requirements, and the organizational structure to support them.

"We spent a lot of time on the goals statement," John van Alstyne noted later. "It's very simple, but we would argue for hours over the use of a certain word. We would look at it from the point of view of all the possible connotations. We wanted a statement that would be clearly a 'motherhood bill'—we wanted it to be so good that everybody would vote for it. Once we had that, then we could go ahead and work on a plan."

Their efforts focused well beyond the WPI community. As Jack Boyd explained, the new program would "make a significant contribution to national educational leadership by providing an educational choice for students interested in scientifically and technologically oriented careers." This was new thinking for "little old WPI in Worcester, Massachusetts," Boyd said in retrospect, "but I think we meant it and I think we have been trying to follow it."

So the goal carefully crafted by the committee became:

It is the goal of Worcester Polytechnic Institute to bring into the second century of its existence a new, dynamic version of its great Two Towers tradition. In its first century WPI pioneered the integration of science and shop; in its second century WPI will pioneer in scientific service to society.

The WPI graduate of the future must have an understanding of a sector of science and technology and a mature understanding of himself and the needs of the people around him. While an undergraduate, he must demonstrate that he can learn and can translate his learning into worthwhile action. He must learn to teach himself those things that are needed to make his actions socially significant. A WPI education should develop a strong degree of self-confidence, an eagerness to contribute to the community beyond oneself, and an intellectual restlessness, a spur to continued learning.

But how to realize this expansive and ambitious goal? Their initial ideas, some of which were scrapped entirely, although many others were refined for later inclusion, bore no resemblance to WPI's existing curriculum. They divided up the work by each member's strengths: Moruzzi calculated how much changes would cost and what the impact on student or faculty numbers might be; Grogan looked at possible curricular structures; Boyd considered student views and suggestions on project work; and Heventhal focused on what a humanities minor could look like.

Heventhal also helped the two Bills see eye-to-eye, as Bill Shipman was more theoretical and graduate student-focused in his training, and Bill Grogan believed the undergraduate program should remain WPI's specific strength. The group worked through a consensus model.

"We never took a vote in that committee, never once," said Heventhal.

The group's summer work put on paper what this radical new way of learning would look like and how it could function. At its core: Taking responsibility for their own education, students would learn how to learn.

"It meant completely turning over everything that we'd done," said Boyd, "and we went a little further than perhaps even we thought would be possible."

They considered the learning environment itself. "Delight in learning is infectious," Boyd had said. How could they develop a program that would inspire students and their classmates to further their intellectual development?

The group reviewed many learning approaches and found the independent study and project combination attractive. Students would be motivated to find what they needed to learn for their projects. The thought was that each student's primary emphasis would be in projects, involving at least 25 percent of his or her academic program.

"Basically, what we needed was a process which involves search, discovery, assimilation, and synthesizing of a variety of ideas," Bill said. "It should involve decision making, and appropriate advice."

One idea was the qualifying project. This would be "not entirely different from a senior thesis," Bill explained, "but a project which was grown so that it could be done in corporate and research lab environments and eventually in different locations in the world."

"Some people may think that [what later came to be known as] the IQP came as a second thought," said Boyd, but for the committee another very basic consideration for student learning was the struggle with the implications of technology. In addition, they sought to help students remain motivated learners, and Boyd noted that "any particular problem becomes interesting once it is recognized as relevant to the student's interests."

For WPI undergraduates to develop an understanding of the interaction between professional concerns and society "seemed to beg for a very different type of experience, on site, if possible," Bill wrote. "This experience would require the solution to a problem at the interface between science and technology on one hand and of social concern and human values on the other. Thus was born what came to be called the 'Interactive Qualifying Project' (IQP) and it would eventually be required of every student. It would have the same time commitment of a quarter of an academic year. In both cases the timing of the work could be arranged in a flexible manner to meet the project's operational requirements."

"Courses would be offered to bring coherence to what has been learned in the projects, and not the other way around," Boyd emphasized. Students would take courses either to supply preliminary information in transition to the new unstructured system at WPI or to learn specific techniques, and then participate in summary courses—lectures for upperclassmen already familiar with the subject from project or other self-study work. Requiring specific courses or numbers of courses to achieve the student learning goal would run counter to the underlying philosophy of the proposed shift to project study.

In addition to the two projects, the committee worked out the concept of a minor or "sufficiency" in the humanities, "but with a choice," clarified Heventhal.

"For many years, humanities offerings at WPI consisted of a choice between history and German," as Bill recounted. "The Planning Committee proposed that WPI should greatly broaden its humanities offerings and present them in a structure to effectively form a five-course humanities minor followed by a capstone requirement."

It's "what I'm most proud of," Heventhal said. "Every student could now choose an area of the humanities or arts they wished to work in, such as literature, history, philosophy, a foreign language, drama-theater, or music. The final course would require a substantial paper to demonstrate the theme and accomplishment of the sequence."

"The objective of this humanities minor," continued Bill, "was the development of knowledge in an area of the humanities to establish for the student a 'sufficient' knowledge base to encourage pursuit of a lifelong enriching experience in the area."

The fourth degree requirement would provide some professional accountability for the degree program. A final exam would evaluate the professional competence of the student nearing graduation. Without a fixed curriculum, Bill wrote, "concern grew in the faculty that, with only the required MQP as the specific determinant of qualification in the student's major field, a comprehensive or 'qualifying' examination in the student's major should also be required for graduation." He explained that the exam "could range from producing and documenting a specified design in the case of engineering majors, or for science majors, research in a designated subject and presenting their results." The exams would be held over a designated week between terms to complete the requirement.

"The faculty liked this," he reported, "as it would improve credibility with the accrediting agencies."

Faculty support for this new approach would also require a shift in reward structure, as guiding students along their learning journey could be quite time-intensive and should be seen as teaching, not merely service.

While the degree requirements were radical enough, the proposed WPI Plan would also include a new grading system, a source of friction within the committee, Bill recounted. "The new philosophy of the Plan held firmly to the proposition that grades were of secondary importance. The purpose of education was to gain knowledge, not marks," he wrote. "Accordingly, the importance of grades was greatly reduced." Most committee members believed "there had to be some attention to achievement level," he said, "but in the temper of the day, we all wanted 'grade grubbing' and intense inter-student competition replaced by a spirit of shared learning and group cooperation in seminars, and especially in group projects." The final proposal included three grades: Acceptable, Acceptable with Distinction, or Not Acceptable.

"What we're trying to develop is in many cases quite controversial," said Boyd, "It's supposed to be based on an unstructured system centered around multidisciplinary, individual, or small group project experiences."

An unstructured system still needed an organizational structure to keep it functioning. What would an ideal organizational chart look like? Years of ideas shared over beers at Bigelow's Tavern returned to the conversation.

The six men began to flesh out on paper how the new program might work. A retreat to the Fitzwilliam Inn in New Hampshire gave them the opportunity to work through some of the logistical challenges. The faculty dean and the new president came up for an after-dinner presentation on their work. They supported the committee's directions.

"I've often thought we should put a plaque up at that inn," Grogan said in an article on the Plan's history. "That's where we really hammered out the Plan."

Their report, "Two Towers III – A Model," distributed in September as scheduled, proposed a central educational goal and combined several of the initial objectives outlined in previous reports. It offered a first view of the novel, project-based curriculum. To graduate, a student would have to complete two independent projects at an advanced level, ideally with one completed off-campus; demonstrate competency in a major area of study through a comprehensive exam; and complete two sufficiency exams that focused on disciplines outside their primary focus. There would be a minimum two-year residency requirement. It also included a suggested organization of the college that restructured it from the ground up to promote interdisciplinary faculty interaction.

The organizational chart they devised eliminated the traditional department structure and replaced departments with three divisions of related study groups. Beneath the president and two vice presidents for academic and external affairs, faculty committees would report to an academic council—a mix of elected and appointed faculty members and students. The council would be overseen by two deans—one for program operations and one for academic resources.

The dean of program operations would be concerned with project administration and research and development initiatives. Division chairmen of study groups would report to the dean of academic resources. For purposes of illustration only, the report grouped together in one division the humanities, government, pure math, and physical education; materials, chemistry, energy, radiation, biology, and optics in another; and electricity, applied chemistry, mechanics, applied math, environmental systems, and economics in a third.

That aspect of the third report, clearly a frontal attack on the department heads, was viewed as far too radical and almost set back the entire process. The committee received a great deal of feedback from their faculty colleagues.

Bill said later, "That organizational chart almost did us in completely. I'd recommend to anyone ever undertaking a planning function again in the future—never, never put an organizational chart in it because people instantly open to that, put names in the boxes, lock up their heads, and that's it."

The initial planning document allocated the longest period of time to developing the model for final discussion and, eventually, a faculty vote. From September 1969 to March 1970, the planning committee's marching orders were as follows:

- Enlarge planning group to include students.
- Complete detailed analyses of "best" objectives.
- Prepare final reports for each objective.
- Prepare proposal for continued planning.
- Report to policy-making agencies of the school.

"Once we got this out before the faculty," van Alstyne recalled, "we got everybody we possibly could involved in smoothing down the rough edges to help us come out with the final form."

Another planning day on October 3, attended this time by 275 students and 150 faculty and staff members, prompted both polite and politically charged discussions, many of which tended to focus on details yet to be proposed. A lottery divided participants among 18 groups, with both faculty and students taking on the roles of moderators and recorders. Planning Committee members joined in the discussions and listened intently.

Opposition to the proposed model came quickly from various faculty factions. In a first for WPI, the faculty petitioned for a meeting on October 22, 1969. The exchange between planning committee members and their faculty colleagues was pointed and direct. Why were such radical changes needed? Have we been such a complete failure, or is that just a matter of opinion? Can undergraduates cope with projects? Won't projects become technically trivial? Won't adding more courses in the humanities necessarily water down the technological basics needed for engineering careers? Why not push off humanities courses until graduate school? Are exams needed if a student successfully completes a project?

To respond to rising concerns, faculty meetings became more frequent.

In a "Faculty Pen" column published in *Tech News* in late October 1969, civil engineering professor Bob Fitzgerald '53 wanted a more measured transition. A member of Bill Grogan's Curriculum Study Committee, he argued that while evolution in education was inevitable in response to social changes, and agreeing that the school needed to change to survive, he felt that a wholesale change to the model outlined in "Two Towers III" would be unwise. In a controlled experiment, the existing and untested approaches could run concurrently.

"We must not totally commit ourselves to any new experimental program before it proves itself to be viable," he wrote, suggesting instead that the Plan "be carried on in addition to, rather than in place of, our existing organization, suitably modified."

A slew of new planning subcommittees with both faculty and student members channeled these many and varied responses to the proposed academic and organizational models. "The Plan was discussed in committee meetings and fraternity house meetings," said Bill. "We met with students of all kinds and types. We included the students in it, because we wanted to get the word from the frontline."

Student interest in joining subcommittees far exceeded expectations, with 174 volunteers signed up, and 90 ultimately placed, joining 74 faculty members. Their reports—on everything from college environment and student life and the overall "psyche" at Tech to general implementation, courses, and examinations (the latter chaired by Grogan)—were due by early December.

For the first half of the 1969–70 academic year, the committee "spent many hours in intense discussion among themselves, and with many faculty and students, individually and in groups," Bill recalled. "We also visited other institutions, received valuable insights from outside experts, and comments from trustees and alumni."

Language describing the Institute's central education goal was amended slightly from the Planning Committee's careful work from the previous summer, and a faculty vote endorsing it on December 17, 1969, gave clearer focus to the overall Plan.

> It is the goal of the Worcester Polytechnic Institute to bring into the second century of its existence a new, dynamic version of its "Two Towers" tradition.

> By means of coordinated programs tailored to the needs of the individual student, it is the fundamental purpose of WPI to impart to the student an understanding of a sector of science and technology and a mature understanding of himself and the needs of the people around him. The WPI student, from the beginning of his undergraduate education, should demonstrate that he can learn on his own, that he can translate his learning into worthwhile action, and that he is thoroughly aware of the interrelationships among basic knowledge, technological advance, and human need. A WPI education should develop in the student a strong degree of self-confidence, an awareness of the community beyond himself, and an intellectual restlessness that spurs him to continued learning.

Beyond the faculty, Bill said, the model was reviewed in subcommittees by "alumni who were executives in corporations so they could see where we were headed. We didn't want to have corporations saying, 'We're not going to recruit at WPI because it's falling behind.' We wanted to be ahead, so we put them on a subcommittee, and we put students on subcommittees, and got their ideas. And it worked like a charm." The inclusive approach helped shape the final form of the Plan.

As they sifted through the mountain of suggestions and fears, a clearer academic program gradually emerged. They planned to present their draft to the trustees in early February.

It had to be an all or nothing proposal, they felt, or it would be too easy for the institution to slide back to its old ways if only a pilot program was undertaken.

With further feedback, their work crystallized into a concrete proposal. The planning committee issued its final report, "Two Towers, Part Four: A Plan," in April 1970. Unlike the first three reports wrapped in standard WPI maroon, they published it with a green cover to encourage the faculty to give it a green light.

MOVING TOWARD A VOTE

With "Two Towers IV" in hand, the committee's work intensified that spring. While the planning document had anticipated that by June

42

30, 1970, they would collect evaluations of alternative objectives from campus groups, reach final recommendation on objectives, and request policy-making agencies of the school to select a specific objective, they had instead blended several of the original objectives, and created a proposal for a faculty vote.

Finalizing how their model would be presented to the faculty for an up-or-down vote required meetings. Lots of them. Bill counted 13 faculty meetings, held twice a week, with each one lasting anywhere from an hour and a half to three hours as the group worked through countless revisions and amendments to the one page of proposals outlined in the report.

"We all worked double time," said Weininger, who at that point served as a consultant to Bill's general implementation subcommittee. "But nobody worked harder than Bill."

Off campus, the spring of 1970 marked a time of social upheaval. The war in Vietnam had spread to Cambodia. Students had been shot at Kent State. Protests, sit-ins, and campus boycotts spread across the country. Even WPI students went on strike, boycotting classes for three days.

Responding to student concerns took more time. As Bill recalled, beyond the faculty meetings, there were "some six or seven other meetings, plus teach-ins, and so forth, that were going on at the same time."

One night, he said, "I got home after one of these meetings about five minutes of twelve and sat down with my wife for a cup of tea. I said, 'Well, at least nothing else can happen today,' and there was an enormous noise outside. Some teenagers coming down the street had crashed into my car and smashed the whole back end. That was kind of a nadir."

Bill was so busy in part because he was so good at his job. As Heventhal recalled from that spring of 1970, "Grogan was terrific with the politics of it all." Much like political campaign strategists, the committee would size up departments and how much support their faculty had for the Plan. "Who else from the department could help us make a breakthrough?" was a recurring question, and Bill Grogan would drop in for a visit with that person, "with all his brains and blarney both," Heventhal said.

"Bill could combine the big vision with the nitty gritty," said Weininger. "He knew there was political work to be done." One of his strengths was that "in the midst of noise and argument, he had a really exquisite sense of the core issue. He could project himself into someone's emotions." He tried, Weininger said, to avoid the typical "us versus them" exchanges in contentious discussions.

As Weininger observed, Bill would intuit that "what was bothering Professor X wasn't what he said. In fact, his contributions had been undervalued, and he could be persuaded. He could turn somebody."

The degree of opposition served as their barometer to the strength of the Plan. To Weininger, "it was excruciating. We were in the trenches. It was muddy, rainy, and we were under fire."

While he was ready to melt down, he said, "Bill was very firm." He rarely banged the table or yelled, but when he was feeling the crunch, he said, Bill's facial expressions would make it clear he was "a boiler under pressure. His eyes narrowed. He had a look of determination—more like a bulldog, the set of his mouth." To those who disagreed with him, Weininger said, it was clear "you aren't going around this guy, you gotta go through him."

THE VOTE

"One of the great debates during the spring centered not around anything in the Plan," Bill recounted. "It was really whether or not the Plan, as proposed, should be undertaken as a sort of sub-college, or a college within, which would not affect the entire Institute. And the question was, should that be the route or should there be a commitment of the entire college and all its resources irrevocably to this new program?"

Because the Planning Committee insisted on an up-or-down vote on a final proposal, the faculty received a compilation of amendments submitted to the secretary of the faculty prior to their presentation and discussion at faculty meetings held on May 12, 13, 15, 18, and 19, 1970. Faculty suggested changes to the graduate studies section, the president's authority to modify the administration or operation of the

Institute, elimination of the controversial organizational structure without departments, and alterations to the calendar of implementation.

When the debates ended and it was time to vote, "there were amazingly few changes considering the amount of discussion," said Bill. Amendments that received majority votes were the requirement to have twelve units of study, equivalent to three years in residence, prior to taking the Comprehensive Exam (submitted by chemical engineer professor Wil Kranich) and 1/3 unit (four terms) of physical education in the first two years to earn an undergraduate degree. The Kranich amendment was critical to the final vote, as it gave more structure to a program whose individually structured learning model appeared somewhat nebulous to its critics.

As agreed, the final vote was by written ballot submitted anonymously before the counting on May 28. The resulting tally, released on May 29, demonstrated that precisely two-thirds of Bill's faculty colleagues were ready to see wholesale changes at WPI.

"It was 92–46 in favor of a total commitment of the college to the new program," Bill said, "and that has been the direction we have taken ever since."

"The vote for the Plan came after the planning committee had offered what the overall curriculum would look like," he said. "It was very hard for some of the older faculty to accept it, because it wasn't specific. It gave broad categories you were supposed to get experience in, but didn't say what the experience should be. And they couldn't tolerate that, they wanted to be told specifics, 'This is what you must do.' We didn't want to do that. We wanted to make it flexible, to allow it to grow with time, to change with new problem situations, make it dynamic.

"And some people resigned. They said, 'That's not the way you teach engineering.' We thought it was the new way of teaching it."

"By turning it inside out," said Weininger, "we turned it around."

CHAPTER THREE

Making It Stick

The fact that the Plan not only survives
but is stronger than ever is Bill Grogan's doing.
—David Riesman

BEFORE THE FINAL vote on the Plan had been taken, President George Hazzard had approached Bill Grogan about accepting a new role, dean of undergraduate studies. That title wasn't in one of the boxes on the controversial organization chart, but its responsibilities covered much of what the proposed dean of program operations would have managed. Reporting to Dean Lawrence "Cookie" Price, Bill would be responsible for the undergraduate curriculum and program planning, summer school, and academic affairs of the growing consortium of Worcester colleges and universities.

President Hazzard's verbal job description was a simple one: "Implement the WPI Plan. And help find the money to do it." Bill agreed, and a memo went out campus-wide on April 14, 1970.

There was no blueprint for Bill to take the conception of the Plan and make it operational. "It was a new position, it had never existed before,"

Above: *As dean, Grogan oversaw the campus-wide implementation of the WPI Plan.*

Bill noted. Having battled the administration for so many years, he felt he had to explain why he took the position, recalled Steve Weininger. "He had extended discussions with the president and provost about his responsibilities, his authority, and means. He was leery of becoming a figurehead."

He was also the first dean who had not served as a department head first. "That made it a little bit harder, not for the faculty, but for the department heads to deal with," Weininger said. "They were good people, despite their reservations about the new programs."

That first year, Bill recalled, "we had a whole list of things that needed to be changed. The very nature of education changed."

His agents of change joined the revolutionary General Implementation Committee (GIC), which gave equal voices to administrative and faculty committee members. Working together with President Hazzard, Bill wanted it to be inclusive, as he explained, "because the Plan has to involve everybody, everybody was affected. Department heads … who wanted to understand their new roles, people from all kinds of representative disciplines, all layers of the campus, including secretaries. The registrar had to be a part of it. The athletic department, for example, would be affected."

As the new plans developed, his approach would keep the campus community informed, and, ideally, quell resistance. Faculty policy committee heads for curriculum, academic policy, student advising, and academic operations joined the registrar, the dean of academic advising, and administrators for placement and continuing education.

"I had about six permanent members, and about ten members that kept rotating," Bill said, "depending upon what the topic of the period was that we had to address." The group met weekly for about 15 years as it addressed multiple challenges to implementing the Plan over time.

"Many of the problems that we had to solve involved academics, involved standards, involved bringing the students in and getting faculty involved—some of whom were excited to do it and some who really didn't want to." At the same time, he said, "we were changing the calendar, changing the grading system, and all of these absolutely required the participation of our administrative staff. They were the ones that were going to make the system run, especially the registrar."

Those first two summers on the job, he said, he also created several ad hoc committees to address specific challenges—and to nurture the passions of the planning committee era. He intentionally kept them small, with no more than three people on each one. "The committees consisted of both students and faculty. We had some students who were on the original planning committee as freshmen who stayed right on and participated in the faculty committees until graduation. It was a very cooperative and extremely interesting period."

Bill found people cooperative, in part, because he skillfully built bridges to those who had not been supporters of the Plan. "They did not identify me yet as an authority figure," he recalled. "So I spent a lot of time out of my office, going to the faculty offices, and I went and visited with the department heads and, in a sense, brought them back into the system again."

Part of his mission, he found, was to give faculty members permission to try new things. "I went to department meetings and told them it was OK. If somebody wanted to do something, I would say, 'Go ahead and try it.' The faculty had been constrained over the years by this rigid structure and my job was to say, 'You go ahead and do it.'"

Bill would ask them, "Does it have intellectual integrity? Is it demanding?" And if their answer was yes, he would say, "Try it. If it doesn't work well, don't do it again.

"Try it, try it, try it. That was my message," he said.

"There was a great tolerance for new ideas," agreed civil engineering professor Bob Fitzgerald '53. "Failure would be accepted."

Few changes were visible to WPI visitors during Bill's first year as dean. For the 1970–71 and 1971–72 academic years, students were allowed to remain in the traditional program. Incoming freshmen could choose the Plan or not, but all students followed a semester calendar that first year. In practice, the school had to run two programs concurrently.

But behind the scenes, a great deal of high-intensity decision making and planning was under way. With a new calendar kicking in for the fall of 1972, every course needed reexamining. Thanks to WPI's initial financial commitment and support from the National Science Foundation, the GIC had summer funding for professors in every department, including physical education, to develop new courses or adapt existing ones to both the new seven-week term length and the new individually paced instruction model. Over time, faculty overhauled more than 400 courses.

The first fruits of these labors appeared in January 1972, when WPI faculty and students participated in the inaugural Intersession. There were a number of goals for this unorthodox curricular approach, Grogan told WPI's alumni magazine. "The idea was to let members of the WPI community try new things, to enable faculty members and students to get to know each other in new combinations, and to give students an opportunity to pick up useful ancillary material they could use in their courses and projects."

In looking back, Bill said, "that was probably the high point of the entire seven-year implementation period. Intersession was universally, enormously popular. The first one was an experience of a type we had never had before in the college. The fact that students and faculty would be standing together having a cup of coffee and talking about something was really mind exploding."

Over a nearly three-week period in January between terms, students, faculty members, and alumni alike had more than 400 mini-courses to choose from. Professors in economics, government, and business, for example, offered sessions on personal finance, the Small Business Administration, solid waste disposal, and law and product liability. More exotic choices included building a house or living in a commune, bachelor cooking, and hot and cold off-campus options to participate in either oceanographic research or winter mountaineering.

The change that was hardest to swallow for many at WPI was the calendar of four seven-week terms, labeled A through D, with a break between each one. Classes would meet four times a week, with one or two additional scheduled labs. "It was a major jolt to the system," Bill said. As the first term began in September 1972, reality set in during

Left: Bill Grogan's parents, William and Irene, on their wedding day in Lee, Massachusetts, in 1923.

Below: Bill and his sister, Mary Elizabeth (Betty), behind the family home in Lee. Born when Bill was four, Betty still recalls Bill's "abundance of confidence."

Bill in an undated photo that was probably
taken during his WPI student years.

Bill learned to play the piano at St. Mary's School in Lee, and enjoyed
playing for friends and family throughout his life.

During his Navy service, Bill looked forward to spending leaves
with his parents, his sister, Betty, and his brother, Edward.

M.I.T. game at the house where festivities of March 31st. when informal dancing and a punch bowl Maurice "Gus" Gosselin will enter

Prof. W. R. Grogan
Tapped for Skull;
Leaves for Navy

Well-liked Classics
To Be Presented

On January 27, 1951, William Robert Grogan. Assistant Professor

A graduate of the Navy's wartime V-12 program, Bill completed two tours of active duty, just after World War II and during the Korean War. Before he left campus, he was tapped for WPI's student honorary society, Skull.

The apprentice seamen in WPI's Navy V-12 program assemble
for a formation on the football field. In the inset, Bill is at the
rear of the second column from the left.

First row, left to right: H. Slaughter; J. Landers, Chapter Sec'y; R. Anschutz, Corresponding Sec'y; C. Simon, President; R. Martin, Vice-President; W. Gleason, Treasurer.
Second row: W. Grogan; R. Chase; W. Wells; G. Nylen; J. Metzger.
Third row: W. Hatch; W. Bergman; J. Hossack; W. Conlin.

Among Bill's numerous activities and academic honors during his WPI years (*below*) was his election to Tau Beta Pi, the engineering honor society (*above*). The society's insignia (*right*) is a watch key in the shape of the supporting frame, or bent, of a trestle bridge.

WILLIAM ROBERT GROGAN
  Theta Kappa Phi, Tau Beta Pi, Sigma Xi
    Lee, Massachusetts

  Electrical Engineering

Tech News 1, 2, 3, 4, Editor-in-chief 4; Debating Club 1; Newman Club 1, 2, 3, 4, Vice-President 3, President 4; A.I.E.E. 2, 3, 4; Photography Editor, PEDDLER 4; S.C.A. Cabinet, Secretary 4; Class Historian 4; Dance Committee 4; Interclass Sports; Radio Club 4; Naval Reserve.

  "Who's Who in American Colleges"

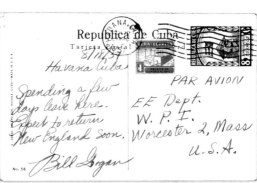

Above: A newly commissioned ensign, Bill, in 1946, completed studies in electronics in San Diego, where this photo was taken.

Right: Deployed again in 1951, he went to sea on the destroyer USS *Stoddard*, starting with a shakedown cruise to Cuba.

Aboard the *Stoddard*, Bill completed a memorable tour of
the Mediterranean, which included a stop in Venice.

Left: Bill was the *Stoddard*'s electronics officer and a member of the cryptoboard, which handled classified information.

Below: He sent his mother this photo of a typical scene on the bridge during a war games exercise. Seen at far right, he wrote that he was getting a bearing on a submarine periscope.

This is what "plane guard" means.

LONG-RANGER—The North American AJ-1 attack-bomber is the biggest aircraft ever built to operate from a carrier. It will carry a heavier bomb load farther, faster and higher than any other carrier-based airplane. The AJ-1 is powered by two Pratt & Whitney Double Wasp engines of 2,300 h.p. each, and a single J-33 jet engine. It is shown here joining up with Vought Corsair fighter-bombers.

Mom In case you wonder what I do and see all day long, this will give you a very good idea. We sail along like this hour after hour ready to pick up any planes that drop off the carrier in landing or taking off. It's very safe indeed for us — but those pilots earn their money — Bill

During Bill's Korean War service, the *Stoddard* took part in numerous maneuvers with the Sixth Fleet. He sent this annotated clipping to his mother to help her visualize his day-to-day shipboard life.

Above: While in Rome, Bill (*second from left*) had two audiences with Pope Pius XII. He sent this medal blessed by the pontiff to a Franciscan cleric and friend.

Below: Orphans enjoy ice cream aboard the *Stoddard* in Salerno, Italy. When Bill later invited aboard the townspeople of Brindisi, he thought he might be court-martialed.

TECH NEWS MAN OF THE YEAR:
Prof. William Robert Grogan

The *Tech News Association* has chosen Prof. William R. Grogan as its W.P.I. Man of the Year. The award is being presented him for his outstanding achievement and exemplary display of character in his association with the Curriculum Study Committee, of which he is Chairman. In spearheading the volum-

inous amount of work necessary for the success of this project, Prof. Grogan has been most responsible for the historic curricula changes which are to be initiated at the Institute in the near future.

We take great pride in announcing Prof. Grogan as our choice for this award.

Prof. William Robert Grogan

Above: Following his Navy deployments, Bill settled into his role as a professor of electrical engineering at WPI. He found WPI's rigid curriculum stifling, but a chance to change it as head of the Curriculum Study Committee kept him at WPI and won him an accolade from the student newspaper (*left*).

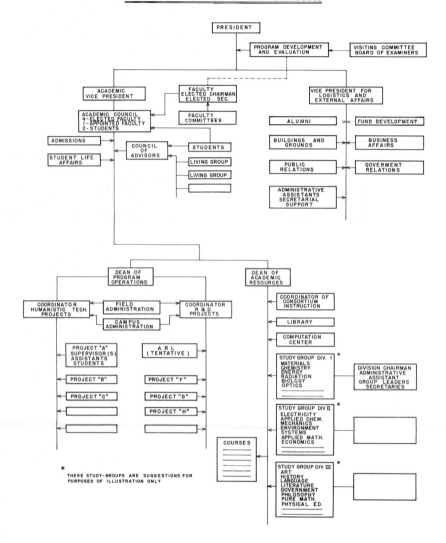

FIGURE I

SUGGESTED ORGANIZATION OF THE COLLEGE

In 1969, Bill was elected to a faculty planning committee that ultimately produced the WPI Plan. In one of the committee's reports it proposed a new organizational structure for the Institute that proved to be too radical. It "nearly did us in," he wrote later.

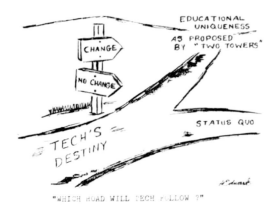

"WHICH ROAD WILL TECH FOLLOW ?"

Left: As the proposal for the WPI Plan took shape in the fall of 1969, *Tech News*, the student newspaper, wondered if the Institute would be bold enough to break from the status quo.

Below: When the program went to the faculty for approval in 1970, a full third voted against it.

WORCESTER POLYTECHNIC INSTITUTE
Worcester, Massachusetts

May 29, 1970

To: WPI Faculty

From: Secretary of the Faculty

Subject: Vote on the Planning Committee Report

Pursuant to action at the May 12, 1970 Faculty Meeting, the final vote on the Planning Committee Report was to be by written ballot. The results follow:

MOTION: To adopt the sections of "The Future of Two Towers, Part IV: A Plan" as presented and amended at the Faculty Meetings of May 12, 13, 15, 18, and 19, 1970.

VOTED:

in favor	92
opposed	46
abstaining	3
total returns	141

Respectfully

James Hensel
Secretary of the Faculty

Even before the Plan vote, President Hazzard asked Bill to become WPI's first dean of undergraduate studies.

From his busy office in Boynton Hall, Bill oversaw the Plan's implementation.

A College Throws Out the Curriculum

By TIM METZ

WORCESTER, Mass.—"Four years from now may well see Worcester Polytechnic Institute heralded as a true innovator in private higher education," says George W. Hazzard, the college's president. "On the other hand, you might see me standing down here on Route 9 with my thumb out."

Mr. Hazzard is partly joking, of course, but he does have reason to wonder what his future holds. Worcester Polytechnic, which he has headed for one year, is about to toss out its entire curriculum and start over. After 18 months of planning and haggling among administrators, faculty and students, the 105-year-old, 2,100-student college has set out to remake itself from a nuts-and-bolts school of engineering to a breeder of scientific humanists who are prepared to bend science directly to social concerns.

The vehicle for this transformation is the "WPI Plan," which will be formally announced tomorrow. The plan is based on two central themes: A complete change in the standards by which a student's progress is measured, and a belief that attempts by engineering students to solve real world problems —even insoluble ones—have far greater academic value than has yet been recognized.

Until this year, a degree at WPI, as at the overwhelming majority of other schools, has represented the accumulation of a prescribed number of academic value units, or credits. A course is assigned a certain number of such credits, or credit hours as they are called by some schools. Degrees have been awarded on the basis of a student's collection of the proper number of credits in various prescribed areas of study, with the mix of credits determined by the department whose degree the student seeks.

Fresh Start for Freshmen

But for freshmen beginning at WPI next year, and for each entering class for three years after that, there will no longer be "credits" to earn, nor will there be prescribed academic programs of courses that students must pursue for a degree in their area of specialty.

Each student's course of study will be determined solely by himself and his faculty adviser.

In place of the accumulation of credits as a path to a degree, the WPI Plan will require both a major off-campus project and a comprehensive examination by the end of the student's career at the school. As currently planned, a student can take the comprehensive exam after he has completed the equivalent-of three years of work.

Students will have wide latitude in selecting off-campus study projects. A faculty member and 15 students will comprise a study project team that will work on one or more engineering problems posed by such "real world" institutions as business and municipal government. In more limited pilot projects over the past several years, WPI students have aided such companies as American Optical Co. and Heald Machine Co. to solve manufacturing and product engineering problems as part of their work in an engineering economics course. "Several of my students have been hired by companies where they worked on these projects while they were here," reports William R. Grogan, the dean of undergraduate students who also teaches the course.

To accommodate the emphasis on such projects under the WPI Plan, the school year will be broken into five seven-week terms. One term, to be conducted over the summer, will stress remedial and other preparatory work for students who come to WPI with an inadequate high school education. As an added effect, the seven-week• academic periods "are certain to make it easier for poor students to move back and forth between jobs and school with the least possible delaying effect on their progress toward a degree," said Mr. Grogan.

As currently envisioned, WPI's civil engineering, chemical engineering and mechanical engineering departments will spearhead the changeover to the WPI Plan, through a liaison with Worcester and other towns and with several industries. Students from their second year onward will be encouraged to become involved in study projects aimed at helping on such issues as air and water pollution, parking and even urban beautification.

While WPI currently has no serious economic problems, the new plan promises to put it on firmer financial footing. With about a quarter of the student body projected to be involved in off-campus study projects each term, college living space and other facilities will be opened to greater full-year use, which should lower costs. And, by working on study projects at business and other facilities away from the campus, students will be using the equipment on the scene, "which should save WPI some money in outlays for exotic new equipment," says a school spokesman. Faculty members, too, will be grouping for maximum efficiency in teaching basic science courses as they relate to the various engineering disciplines. In math, for example, some subjects, such as advanced algebra, will be taught with once-weekly lectures in a large hall, followed by smaller meetings during the week in which an instructor relates the week's lesson to his own group's special field of engineering.

This expected more efficient use of faculty and facilities should let the school enroll up to 500 more students with minimal bricks-and-mortar additions and without enlarging the faculty. It has been projected that the switch to the WPI Plan will cost the school about $2 million over the next four years, or about 5% of the projected operating budget over that span.

Why did Worcester Polytechnic make the switch? Like many other private schools, WPI is learning that nearby state schools "can do a fine job of turning out graduate engineers using the same kind of classical approach to the subject we have been using all these years," says Romeo L. Moruzzi, a WPI professor of electrical engineering.

"The question then becomes, how much longer should students be willing to pay us $2,400 a year to do essentially what the University of Massachusetts can do for $200 a year?" he says. "If private schools can't offer something unique in education, then they really have little reason to exist."

Difficulties Ahead

Nobody at WPI pretends the change will be easy. All agree that the faculty's commitment to the new concept will be crucial. "The usual ivory-tower professor does not generally qualify" to teach under the WPI Plan, says Carl C. Koontz, who heads WPI's civil engineering department. "The need is for people-oriented engineers, not engineering-oriented people."

And faculty cooperation is far from assured. At a June meeting nearly a third of the school's then 152 faculty members voted to turn down the WPI Plan, though a few of them said they did so because they felt it wasn't radical enough. M. Lawrence Price, dean of faculty, spent the summer screening a list of more than 600 prospective faculty members to replace 10 who left and to add eight, all in the humanities.

Students, too, must react positively to make the plan work. WPI officials are well aware that their plan offers wide latitude to students, and they expect some students to abuse that latitude.

Even if the WPI Plan functions up to expectations, the school may come under fire from outside. "There is some possibility that we could face accreditation problems from our more conservative peers in engineering education, and there's the chance that our graduates under the WPI Plan may want to go on for graduate work at schools which might not honor all their course and project work here," says one liberal arts professor.

Whatever the outcome, little Worcester Polytechnic Institute must be credited with developing a truly innovative approach to higher education and having the grit to implement it. So, if you should happen to spot a middle-aged, bookish-looking man in a cap and gown hitchhiking on U.S. 9 in Worcester a few years hence, pick him up. He'll deserve the lift.

Mr. Metz, a member of the Journal's Boston bureau, is no stranger to the college campus. He holds B.A. and M.A. degrees and is currently pursuing an M.B.A. He also taught freshman English for two years.

As dean, Bill became a spokesman and evangelist for the Plan, helping draw recognition and support for WPI's innovation through his comments to the national media (*top*) and numerous talks to foundations and industry and professional organizations (*bottom*, with President George Hazzard, *second from left*).

the second week. "Within ten days people were going around with petitions, the student newspaper had blanks to fill out, it was very wild," said Bill. "We never realized before what a glacial start the fall term usually had. The bookstore did approximately what they did before, and about the third and fourth weeks people would stop around to pick up the text books. ... Now the term was half over after three weeks. The whole system had to be tightened up enormously."

"It really increased the intensity of the studying that went on," Bill noted, "but one of the principles of the Plan was that the students would take more responsibility for their education. They wouldn't be told everything they had to know ... they would have to fill in the gaps."

The seven-week term also meant that students took only three courses. This would give them enough time to focus on project work, usually undertaken as part of a group of three. A more open schedule for all made it possible to coordinate more group meetings.

At the end of that first A-Term, Romeo Moruzzi, who had replaced Cookie Price on an interim basis as dean of the faculty, hosted a cocktail party for "the beleaguered faculty," as Bill described his colleagues. Held at Higgins House, the mansion recently donated to the school by descendants of one of WPI's first faculty members, the party gave them all a chance to release some of their near-hysteria from teaching at a double-time pace. "It was one of the wildest times we ever had. The faculty were absolutely beside themselves," Bill related. "There has never been an event like it in the history of the Institute."

Many of the new courses offered that year were highly interdisciplinary, which the Plan encouraged with Bill's support. Some courses were now described as studies, others were study-conferences (S-C)—a combination of lecture, small group discussion, and laboratory work where appropriate. New choices included "Introduction to Environmental Problems," "Introduction to Engineering Problems," and "Music of Western Civilization." Other new topics listed for 1972 included "American History for Foreign Students," "Introduction to Art," "Nuclear Physics," "Sanitary Engineering," and "Transportation and Earth Science."

To help fulfill the new graduation requirement, the Physical Education Department offered an introduction to lifetime sports, including golf, tennis, swimming, squash, bowling, volleyball, badminton, and table tennis. Students could learn how to coach football or basketball, or qualify as an aquatics instructor or program supervisor.

Students could access new forms of information for their studies by checking out videotapes from the library. As part of individually pre-scribed instruction (IPI), they could review taped lectures and other sources in course book format, prepared in advance by the faculty.

As Bill explained to the National Science Foundation in 1974, the Plan retained certain traditional elements of education. "We definitely have individual curricula," he said, "as we well appreciate that in scientific and engineering education, there is a hierarchy of learning that is inescapable. Despite this constraint, however, there is still remarkable flexibility in the way students can put together individual programs."

"I think we've come out with a rather simple axiom," he would say to all naysayers, "responsible students will accept responsibility and can do it."

In the long run, Bill noted, "the students loved the seven-week term and the graduates liked it. They said it was tremendous preparation for their careers, because their jobs in industry or laboratories followed that kind of high-intensity, short-term push. More than anybody else, they were prepared to cope with it."

MANY PROJECTS AND WHERE TO FIND THEM

After that first Intersession, Bill said, "we started to gear up our project activity."

Before 1972, there had been 63 project registrations. But the math started to generate some scary numbers. "It was fairly easy to see that with approximately 400 to 500 seniors, each with a minimum of two qualifying projects, we would have over 800 project registrations yearly," said Bill. "Plus, we hoped, a lot more undergraduates taking projects on a preliminary basis before they took the qualifying projects." While students did not register for preliminary projects as anticipated, in 1972 750 students were involved in 630 projects; in 1973 those numbers hit Bill's target, ballooning to 1,300 students in 800 projects.

One of the great worries Bill shared was "where in the world were we ever going to get enough ideas for all these projects?" In his years as dean he had often said, "There have been mornings when I woke up at 4 a.m. and said, 'My God, what have we done?' as I wondered how we're ever going to be able to make it all work."

But he was grateful for "a tremendous outpouring of energy throughout this period on the part of the faculty and a great deal of support on the part of the students." Alumni proved to be a fertile source of projects in their businesses. And to be successful learning experiences on cooperation, leadership, and synthesis of ideas, projects needed to be undertaken by groups of students, ideally three, which significantly reduced the total number of projects required.

Identifying enough high-quality projects turned out to be an unnecessary worry, because, as Bill noted, "the projects breed new ideas for projects, and we now have calls from industry and other places suggesting projects to us and no shortage of project ideas." In those first years, WPI published a thick volume with hundreds of project options each year for students to select from.

Project involvement benefited faculty as well as students. Because projects are "always addressing new problems," Bill said, they "keep the faculty right up to date. So it's a very dynamic system."

The grading system remained as proposed with a slight alteration. Passing grades were acceptable or acceptable with distinction. Rather than giving a student "non-acceptable," they instead received an NR, or No Record. The intention was to encourage exploration of subjects outside their primary interests. Why penalize someone for reaching too high only to learn they need more background for that course? "We do not give F grades," Bill said. "We give No Records because a transcript should be a record of accomplishment and not a record of failure."

"It was a system that kept encouraging you to accomplish something," said Paula (Fragassi) Delaney '75, a member of the first class to enroll in the Plan as freshmen, a group that called themselves the "Plan babies."

It was a constant learning process during those first years, Bill said. "The things I thought would be the worst problems turned out not to be, and the things I didn't realize were lying there then surfaced and turned out to be really big problems. But it wasn't all bad. I had some very positive support."

Bill was constantly mindful of the fact that while the Plan had passed with a two-thirds faculty vote, a less supportive one-third either resigned from WPI or remained resigned to participating in its implementation "in the spirit of the Plan." But he was always grateful for the academic culture of respect among faculty at WPI, which many visitors commented on as they came to learn more about the Plan and its implementation.

"The culture at WPI was one of politeness and mutual respect, and I tried to encourage that," said Bill. "It wasn't that hard. There were people that I had a lot of arguments with that really did not believe that this was the way to go. ... We would have big arguments. But I must say through that whole thing no personal animosity developed. It was on principle."

Regarding one opponent in particular, Leighton Wellman, who had submitted the Curriculum Study Committee's minority report and fervently wanted to keep the drawing requirement, Bill said: "He was a very good friend of mine. ... We did not agree on the concepts of education that we each espoused, but we were always good, personal friends."

Bill found that a division into thirds was true "with any new adventure: the third who want it and will do anything to get it; the third who really didn't want it and would love to see it scuttled; and the middle third who want to be on the winning side."

Reinforcing the Message

As Bill and the GIC labored to erect the new structure for the undergraduate curriculum at WPI, the school's public relations, publications, and fund-raising professionals went into high gear. WPI needed to attract new students to enroll in its untested program, and it needed funding to pay for all the costs incurred by the long list of changes. The trustees had made it clear that beyond an initial investment to launch the Plan, they would not support a program that increased operating expenses.

A new fact sheet spelled out its distinctive features. A new admissions booklet highlighted the power it put in students' hands. President Hazzard was ready for interviews. He wasn't above writing his own articles either. And Bill Grogan was happy to provide a vivid quote.

The national media noticed.

The Wall Street Journal, a publication Bill considered required daily reading, was the first national publication to pay attention to WPI's revolutionary shift. On October 2, 1970, it published the intriguing headline "A College Throws Out the Curriculum" the day before WPI made the official announcement of its change to the Plan.

"Tech School Students Plan Own Programs," announced the *Los Angeles Times* as the school year was getting under way in 1972. The reporter listened to Bill's careful explanations of how students would learn in the new program, and how it served to replace a woefully outdated system of course requirements. "Bright kids used to come here with pet projects they wanted to work on. We'd tell them, 'No, you put that aside until you've taken math and chemistry and physics and so on.' They wouldn't do it and we'd flunk them out. That was pretty dumb." His words were reprinted in wire stories nationwide.

The New York Times' annual education review in January 1973 featured Hazzard's article on how his school was trying to "mold a broader, more humanistic graduate" through projects that help engineers understand the social context for technological advances.

The president also submitted articles to a number of professional organization publications in engineering so engineering professionals and hiring managers could understand WPI's decisions and new methods of instruction.

"Free but accountable," declared the *Christian Science Monitor's* summary of the Plan in 1971, referring to student choice not tuition costs. In a 1973 article titled, "It's Your Education," the National Science Foundation, a major funder of the Plan since its inception, featured WPI in its magazine *Mosaic* as one of three institutions that were handing students more responsibility for their education.

A writer from *Newsweek*'s Boston bureau penned "WPI's Program for Technological Humanists" for *Change* magazine in 1974, outlining the story of a freshman already bored with his required engineering courses, but fired up with enthusiasm a year later after throwing himself fully into project work and advanced urban planning courses. Bill described the effects on both students and faculty. "A lack of rigid structure creates anxiety for teachers as well as students. For many of the old teachers it's a matter of teaching old dogs new tricks ... but on the whole there is an acceptance of the reality that it is possible to learn and learn well without being told it in class."

BusinessWeek waited to see more results before publishing "Engineers Learn by Doing" in August 1974, the month before all freshman and sophomore students would be fully enrolled in the Plan. "Projects, not classwork, are the major vehicles for learning," was Bill's executive summary for the reporter.

The attention, while not always glowing, did help the school build its case with funding sources. President Hazzard was a "genius fundraiser," Bill said, and he made a convincing case with foundations that had never supported engineering schools before that WPI was offering the "new, fuller liberal arts education." The study of liberal arts did not provide the dimension of technology, and WPI was addressing what many people thought was a great omission.

"I remember going with President Hazzard to all kinds of society meetings, national educational meetings where WPI had never been represented before," Bill said. "This included the National Association of Higher Education, which had attendance from almost all the major foundations. We made the presentation of our new concept of a liberal arts college, and I can remember George Hazzard standing outside the elevator shaking hands with the heads of these foundations as they came out and offering to meet with them to discuss our ideas."

Ultimately, critical funding for the Plan came from the National Science Foundation, the Sloan Foundation, the Rockefeller Foundation, the Carnegie Foundation, the Mellon Foundation, the National Endowment for the Humanities, and several corporate foundations.

One pivotal use of NSF funding was for a three-day orientation every summer for the new faculty. It was time well spent.

"Three days!" exclaimed Paula Delaney, who worked with Bill as a student employee organizing the orientation program and later returned to WPI as registrar. "Well, if your only experience is semesters, non-projects, you've been to graduate school, you've got your doctorate, you are walking into something that is very different," she said. "Bill knew it was important to explain and discuss and show and indoctrinate the new faculty into this different educational model."

Early Impact and Assessments

When the NSF awarded WPI $733,400—the largest College Science Improvement Program (CoSIP) grant to that point—to help underwrite its transformation under the Plan, the agency was "very emphatic about evaluating the results of the Plan," Bill said. Sponsoring a 10-year program, with the majority of the funds to be used from 1972 to 1978, the NSF requested a study of the impact of the Plan on WPI students while in school and as young alumni. The foundation also asked for a comparative study of educational change and progress at WPI and at two peer institutions (Clarkson University and Stevens Institute of Technology) over three years.

Even more useful for Bill and his colleagues was the ongoing feedback from the advisory panel of esteemed scholars and educators appointed by the NSF to monitor their grants: Lee Harrisberger, dean of science and engineering at the University of Texas; Bruce Mazlish, professor of history and head of humanities at MIT; George Pake, vice president for research at Xerox Corporation; Kenneth Picha from the School of Engineering at the University of Massachusetts; Eugene Reed, executive director of the Ocean Systems Division at Bell Telephone

Laboratories; and John Whinnery from the Department of Electrical Engineering at the University of California. Chief among the members was David Riesman, Henry Ford II Professor of Social Sciences at Harvard University, who had spent his career researching innovations in American higher education.

"This was a stellar group, and their reports provide the most interesting and objective commentary on the development of the Plan," said Bill. Issued in 1982, "their final report, which was edited by Riesman, is really the best evaluation we have of the overall education implementation of the WPI Plan."

The early student impact and comparative study was undertaken by Karen Cohen of the Center for Educational Research and Development in Cambridge (who, in a fortunate coincidence, happened to be a neighbor of Steve Weininger at the time).

The school worked with Jeffrey Bock of MIT to evaluate the impact on early career development for WPI students contrasted with a national sample. They also worked with Jack Gabarro '61 of Harvard Business School and Frank Baker of State University of New York at Buffalo on the effects of the early days of the Plan on faculty health and mental well-being. Other studies examined WPI's experience with the IQP five and ten years into the Plan.

Cohen found that WPI graduates were far more self-assured, adventuresome, and willing to take risks, and that they enjoyed the job of digging into and solving problems rather than simply analyzing them. They also liked educational challenges, and a higher percentage of WPI students were interested in pursuing graduate education. Their one deficit was math. More than half felt less comfortable using mathematics in problem solving than their peers.

"Looking back to the pre-Plan education of engineers in general, including WPI," said Bill, "there was a feeling that you never really knew enough to be able to solve an engineering problem ... you could never learn enough to be able to do it right." Those who came to WPI in the Plan's first days displayed a self-confidence their predecessors would have marveled at.

74

When the Plan was fully implemented in 1977–78, another round of national stories addressed WPI's novel program and the interdisciplinary projects undertaken by its students. This time, the reporters could include the initial evaluations the Plan had received from outside reviews, notably the NSF review committee and the research it sponsored on the Plan's impact on recent graduates.

In their estimation, the Plan had launched WPI into the national league. "This position has been earned and is deserved," wrote Riesman in a detailed letter to Bill from July 1978. "When I first began my connection to WPI (and would in an educational meeting use those three letters), almost no one would know what I was talking about unless I made a fuller explanation; now, in general, people do know."

Long after the NSF funding ended, and the Plan had gone through significant revisions, Riesman gave enormous credit to Bill for the longevity of the Plan when so many other experiments like it faded with time. In a tribute to Bill on his retirement in 1990, he wrote, "At first glance, he seems a most unlikely sage of liberal education. He is genial, ruddy, generous, never sarcastic, amiable—everyone calls him 'Bill' almost instantly. Yet in my judgment the fact that the Plan not only survives but is stronger than ever is Bill Grogan's doing."

Growing Technological Humanists

"People will tell you—and studies have been done—that there is something different about a WPI education," Delaney said. When WPI graduates start a new job, their questions reflect their attitude, she said. "There's no 'I can't do that.' Instead, they say, 'when do we start?' There's no 'I'm going to do that on my own,' it's 'who's going to be on my team?' We had all that problem solving and a focus on why we were doing things this way. We were doing this to make the world a better place."

Those differences became very clear to Delaney during one particular term. She and her sister, a student at Assumption College at the time, were both taking embryology classes. "For her test, she was memorizing the Latin names of the parts of the fetus," Delaney recalled. "I was studying what happens when you take one of the cells out of the blastula. We were doing research, asking questions." Would the other cells pick up where it left off? her group asked. Could you even clone it? "Very, very different."

"They taught us how to go and research something, figure out what we needed to know," she said. "We had to consider social, political, environmental questions, what resources were available for everything we were working on. We learned to ask those questions. So when people would ask us what was different, we would say 'well, they taught us how to learn.'"

The tradition has changed, she said, but "what hasn't changed is those goals—learning how to learn, the curriculum being encouraging rather than being punitive. The application of the theory immediately, believing we can make this better. In a way that's what Bill did. He looked at WPI and said 'I can make this better.' And we felt like if we can do this, then we can do so much more."

Not every faculty member could adapt to this different approach to teaching. "One colleague told me he just could not work on a project where students knew more than he did," recalled Weininger. As Weininger saw it, his job was "to ask questions and press them. It was a great way to teach. The students became our junior colleagues."

With the shorter terms, said Frank DeFalco '58, professor of civil and environmental engineering, "We had to revise all our courses and lab courses. You had to decide what you really want to do. I liked the shorter seven weeks, as with only three courses students could concentrate more."

"There are many things we learned from implementing the WPI Plan," reflected Bill. "The first one is, don't get discouraged with the initial reactions to change. They're almost always doubtful, and full of caveats. If you want to change it, go ahead and work through those, and it will happen. That's one of the major things to do. Don't get discouraged at the initial opposition, the initial problems, the unexpected costs. All these things are going to happen. Expect them. But stay with it, and you can work through it."

PROJECTS BEYOND WORCESTER

That thick volume of project possibilities could sit on Bill Grogan's desk in Boynton Hall, but the work involved in executing them needed a space of its own. With funding from the Kresge Foundation and IBM— and a host of volunteer carpenters—the Project Center opened on the third floor of the Washburn Shops in 1973. While the administration was on campus, many of the projects weren't. Initial expectations were for teams of students to work at local industries to solve their "back burner" problems, challenges the company staff did not have time to tackle, much like those in Bill's engineering economics class. But when the project ended, the students would return to campus.

In 1971 the U.S. Army's Natick Labs offered a fertile source for projects. About a half-hour's drive from Worcester, it became the site of the first non-residential off-campus project center, staffed by a WPI director to manage incoming student project teams. By 1975 there were four more in Massachusetts—at Digital Equipment, Norton Company, the Small Business Administration, and St. Vincent's Hospital. Further afield, Bill and the GIC had hoped to establish other on-site corporate project centers, but after visits to U.S. Steel in Cleveland, General Electric in Schenectady, and DuPont in Wilmington, Delaware, Bill found that all the proposed sites would narrow projects to specific disciplines and challenge faculty resources. So the idea faded, only to return in a different form in 1974 with the Washington, D.C., Project Center.

The degree requirements voted by the faculty had included two projects, one of which would be in the major field of study. The second project, however, needed further definition. In 1971 Bill asked chemical engineering professor Imre Zwiebel to head up an interdisciplinary committee. Its charge: Clarify what a project that touched upon "the relationship between science, technology, and society" might look like.

The Zwiebel Committee spent close to a year hammering out the definition and the underlying philosophy behind the second project, which they christened the Interactive Qualifying Project, or IQP. Not just presenting an engineering problem to solve, the IQP would have students encounter a social problem. Once they drafted an initial proposal, they would need different tools for this type of project—survey design, interview skills, and an understanding of community outreach techniques, among many others.

Advising these types of projects required different skills from the faculty as well, and most at WPI did not feel they could take on the task without some training. The Sloan Foundation helped underwrite two summer sessions, held at a scout camp in nearby Spencer. "We were successful in getting some very high-ranking and important individuals to acquaint the faculty with the problem areas and procedures in looking at IQP topics," Bill recalled.

Students could undertake IQPs far beyond Worcester, and the NSF funding helped advance the discussion within the GIC. The $733,400 grant included a line item of $65,000 for an off-campus residential project center. If the projects undertaken there were IQPs, those disciplinary limitations would be lifted, greatly increasing the number of potential locations. WPI settled on Washington, D.C., a place described by physics professor Tom Keil as "rich in a whole range of societal and political issues relating to technology."

After Bill and many colleagues tapped their professional networks to identify sponsoring agencies for projects, the school leased one floor of a building with housing for two faculty advisors and 20 students, along with some meeting rooms. Thus, the Washington Project Center was born. Its success led to establishing other centers in cities across the U.S. and, starting in London in 1987, at dozens of locations overseas.

As it expanded in geographic reach, the Plan remained under constant pressure to change. Requests to scrap the seven-week terms and return to semesters were constant from certain departments. One alteration was made to the grading system. Concerns from graduate schools and prospective employers rose in pitch to protest the lack of recognizable letter grades, or any information about a student's GPA or class standing. Although WPI held off for 15 years, eventually the faculty voted to change to an A/B/C grading system, retaining the No Record (NR) designation for courses not successfully completed.

"I felt the grading system was one of the few mistakes we made," Bill said in an article on implementing the Plan. "It was a compromise between those who wanted a pass/fail system, which would have made it impossible for students to go on to graduate school, and those who wanted a conventional system. It was an experiment that was worth trying, but we held on to it for too long."

Also under close scrutiny was the Competency Exam.

Confronting the Unfamiliar as an Educational MRI

On a Friday afternoon when the Comp results were announced, happy seniors would bound down the stairs to the Goat's Head Pub, screaming, "I'm Competent! I'm Competent!" They had endured a week of grueling written and oral questioning and problem solving—and prevailed. Nothing else stood between them and graduation.

This terminal exam, the fourth degree requirement agreed to in the Plan, had always played a role in the overall discussion of how to determine whether students had met the education goals for an undergraduate degree. Initially described in "Two Towers III: A Model," the exam could be both oral and written, should be of the "open library type," and should be designed in such a way that students could not cram for it. "The student's efforts must not be oriented toward passing the examination. Comprehensive problems, research proposals, design problems, and comparative work are suggested possibilities. In any case, the examination should confront the student with the unfamiliar."

Between the passage of the Plan and its first administration, the exam's name and underlying purpose had shifted from comprehensive to competency. "It was a terrible word for the examination to begin with," declared Bill. "It should have been called Qualifying Examination, since we had Qualifying Projects. The problem with the Competency Examination was that if someone failed it we had the fathers in here saying, 'I paid thousands of dollars to have my son declared incompetent.' That was a very bad strategic point."

Seen as both a sword of Damocles and a spectacular rite of passage,

Bill said "the Comp" was the great common experience shared by more than 7,000 WPI graduates from 1973 to 1986. But like snowflakes, no two were alike. Each exam was customized for the student taking it. And departmental administration of the exams varied widely—from a three-day, open-book, take-home exam to 14 days of programming or a 50-hour open-ended theoretical mathematical problem followed (after a day's rest) by a 90-minute blackboard exam.

The Planning Committee originally saw this degree requirement as "something that would be easily implemented," Bill reflected. "It didn't seem to be all that difficult because a hallmark of a professor is to give examinations. If there is anything that is easy to do, it is to make a competency exam to assess the ability of the student to perform effectively in their professional field at the baccalaureate level. This, however, was the greatest underestimation of difficulty in the entire concept of the WPI Plan."

In its original conception, he said, "we looked at different ways of administering it. There was support for having the exam at the end of the sophomore year, dwelling on engineering and science fundamentals. But that was rejected, as the original concept was to see if the graduate could handle a comprehensive problem in engineering or science at a level commensurate with earning a bachelor's degree.

"Some faculty went to ingenious ways to construct a problem, but even the best ran out of these ideas. Everyone had an idea for the right problem, but once they used it, it was a hard act to follow. It was like the writers who were going to start a new magazine. It was easy for the first and second editions, but by the third they ran out of ideas."

The first exams were administered in 1973 to students who elected into the Plan requirements as upperclassmen. But concerns about the Comp exam were raised early on. In 1976 Bill could honestly tell the new faculty gathered before him, "The competency examination looked like a rather simple thing to give. It's turned out to be our biggest nightmare."

"It worked very well when we had small numbers of students," Bill said later. But then "the percentage of students failing the Comp became a constant, like pi. No matter how many took it, no matter what the department was, it was right around 30 percent every single time the examination was given."

The results had pulled the curtain back to reveal what students actually learned, retained, and applied from their courses. "Many of us became increasingly concerned about the cause of the failure, the exam's validity, and our ability to deal effectively with failed students," he wrote in a retrospective article on the exam. "Some students had top grades in all the courses they might be expected to take, but could not handle a comprehensive problem."

The situation offered a problem worthy of its own Competency Exam. "We had in the Comp an educational MRI that could have provided us with an unparalleled, once-in-a-lifetime opportunity to look into ourselves and relate the outcome to our teaching process and to our goals," wrote Bill. But external funding—and perhaps the will to look quite so deeply at this aspect of the school's performance—was unavailable.

In the end, the accreditors sounded the death knell for the exam by insisting on distribution requirements to ensure that fundamental knowledge was a part of every WPI undergraduate's education. In an example of the law of unintended consequences, Bill said, students would make strategic course selections to improve the likelihood of passing the competency exams the first time. Counter to the Plan's original intent, the exam was minimizing the breadth of their academic exposure. To achieve that balance once again, and to satisfy the accrediting agency, the faculty agreed in another historic vote, on April 10, 1986, to replace the exam with distribution requirements.

GROGAN V. ABET

Any revolutionary change in education will eventually bump up against the standards bearers—those organizations that determine whether a school meets their expectations and is thus worthy of their seals of approval. For WPI, that organization was the Accreditation Board for Engineering and Technology, or ABET, which examined and certified the school's chemical, civil, electrical, and mechanical engineering degree programs.

ABET's requirements in the early 1970s were quite specific: they expected students in accredited engineering programs to have at least a half-year each of science, math, and design, and a year of engineering science. "None of these were specified within WPI's performance-based program," Bill wrote in an article on what he called "the ABET saga."

But ABET guidelines also encouraged experimentation, he noted. WPI faculty and administrators thought that "if by the time the degree was awarded, the graduates could do everything that the graduates of the ABET-prescribed program could do—and hopefully more—then equivalency would be established." Unfortunately for WPI, ABET did not see it that way, at least not in the end.

The first visit by the ABET accrediting team occurred in 1976, as the Plan was nearing full implementation. Eager to learn more about the revolutionary program, ABET sent a blue-ribbon visiting committee, including two members of the National Academy of Engineering and several university presidents. After reviewing MQPs and Competency Exam results, Bill said, "they thought our program was tremendous." ABET awarded the school a full six-year reaccreditation.

In 1982, the visiting team did not have such senior, experienced members. "A more traditional" team, wrote Bill with some disappointment, didn't understand what the Plan was accomplishing. "They examined transcripts in detail, compared them with ABET's distribution criteria, and determined there was significant variance in expected course completions." Reaccreditation was given for only three years, and another team scheduled a visit for 1984 to see what changes WPI would make.

"A long series of—let us say—discussions took place between WPI and ABET on the matter of recognizing experimentation in engineering education in accordance with ABET's guidelines," Bill recounted.

At one point, he attended a meeting of the Accrediting Association in Philadelphia and was asked to speak about the accreditation process. His response was blunt. "I told them about the fact they looked at the small details of the program, and not at the overall scope of what we're trying to do. And I said, 'Unless ABET, the accrediting board, takes a different look at its role in engineering, in science education, it may well end up getting the reputation as the dead hand on American engineering education.'" His comments did not receive a positive response, he said, with the audience actually booing. "I was practically chased out of Philadelphia."

WPI had taken ABET at its word, and after the glowing reviews of 1976, felt supported in the direction it was taking. That made the 1982 report seem all the more harsh. The faculty agonized over their response to ABET's critique, and eventually gave all departments the option to establish 10 units (30 courses or the equivalent work in projects) of distribution requirements in designated areas, broadly defined, such as math and science. The engineering departments would thus meet the ABET criteria, for students entering the class of 1988.

But the 1984 visit did not go well. Unhappy that the faculty had taken two years to establish any distribution requirements, ABET now asked for further tightening of the curriculum to meet more precisely its criteria. "The practical effect was that, by expanding the specific requirements, the flexibility of the overall program was further reduced," Bill explained.

The return of distribution requirements to the WPI curriculum had replaced, albeit in less creative formats, the role of the Competency Exam to demonstrate knowledge of the fundamentals of engineering. Thus it was less difficult for the faculty to vote to eliminate the much-feared exam. Many on campus still mourned its passing, and a group of students paraded an empty coffin labeled "The Plan" outside the room where the vote took place.

"Whether it is still appropriate to call WPI's present educational program 'The WPI Plan' is a matter of personal interpretation," Bill wrote in his August 1986 *WPI Journal* article. "Most of it is in place and thriving, but the original open curriculum, to the extent that it actually existed, is now largely constrained. Still, the unique degree qualifications … do indeed produce for our graduates a broad educational experience with many of those qualities sought in 'Two Towers IV.'"

WPI, and Bill Grogan, may have had the last word in their dispute with ABET. In 1996, the organization completely revamped its accreditation criteria to focus on student learning outcomes instead of their course selections. "So, strange as it may seem," Bill said with some satisfaction, "the accreditation system looks more like WPI's degree requirements now."

The battles to change the grading system, reintroduce distribution requirements, and eliminate the Competency Exam for all students led many people to believe the Plan was dead. But the spirit of the Plan's primary goal of helping students learn how to learn persisted in the projects, increasingly undertaken overseas, where students learned how to learn in other cultural contexts and confront the unfamiliar in another way.

PROGRESS AND PERILS OF THE PLAN

Bill Grogan continued as dean of undergraduate studies until his retirement in the summer of 1990. In August 1989, before the start of his final academic year, he penned a seven-page memo to his faculty colleagues and academic and executive staff members. Titled "Undergraduate Education at WPI: Initiatives & Perils," it included Bill's usual update on the incoming class, student-focused initiatives, WPI's overall competitive position, and the tuition-driven financial picture.

He applauded the work of the admissions and financial aid teams, faculty, staff, and alumni as the school prepared to welcome the second largest freshman class in its history, with more than 700 enrolled and a record 80 transfers. This accomplishment was particularly notable in the face of declining numbers of 18-year-olds coupled with their sudden and dramatic decline in the pursuit of science and engineering careers.

Remaining a true believer, he also gave the Plan credit for the school's success, writing, "Behind it all lies the WPI Plan, which makes WPI absolutely unique in the world of undergraduate engineering and science education. After two decades of commitment, recognition is developing!"

While decades had passed since his first days as dean, the challenges for 1989–90 remained familiar: course scheduling, curriculum review at the freshman and sophomore levels, support for choice of major and struggles with math and science, accreditation, greater student-faculty interaction, and improved project quality. Even the return of ROTC (Air Force this time) entered his discussion. Newer themes were international scholars and global projects in the humanities, summer programs abroad, sorority rush schedules, and community outreach to boost interest in studying science and engineering.

Under the heading "Perils," Bill noted that "only a first-rate undergraduate program can find a market at the rates we charge." He highlighted how dependent faculty salaries are on undergraduate tuition, how few overhead dollars from federal grants are directed to the operating budget, and how many faculty members are researching more and teaching less.

Given that demographic and career trends were not positive for WPI in the long run ("the wolf cries are not empty" and recent admissions success should not lull the school into complacency), he supplied a forecast for tuition and financial aid demands that projected financial aid representing more than a third of all tuition income by 1998, without the development of other sources of income.

Bill ended his memo on a cautious note with his hallmark humor. "WPI has faced rough challenges in the past, and has come through them with ingenuity and strength. However it is accomplished, WPI will do it again—but it would be good to become ingenious fairly soon."

WPI's strength in the face of those demographic headwinds did not go unnoticed. Two months after Bill's last "state of the undergraduate program" memo, *U.S. News & World Report*, in October 1989, named WPI the number one regional college and university in the north, topping 169 others, including Villanova University, Simmons College, and Rochester Institute of Technology. Winning features included recognition by its peers as "one of the finest undergraduate engineering schools in the nation," the quality of its faculty, selective admissions, high-scoring freshman SATs, stable enrollment, and the second highest per-student endowment for the region.

The magazine also highlighted WPI's "energetic" recruitment efforts, including building math and science skills for area K-12 students through tutoring, teacher training, and science fairs.

Whether the Plan was alive or on campus in spirit only, as Bill Grogan neared his well-deserved retirement, his supporters could fairly claim WPI's successes as the result of his unyielding efforts to provide an education where students learned how to learn and could translate their learning into worthwhile action.

Honorable Work

Bill's work to implement the Plan and keep WPI moving forward as the Plan evolved over the span of two decades won him recognition from many quarters. Visitors to his office or, in later years, to his home office, would marvel at the accolades covering his wall, "kind of like a museum," as a young fraternity officer once said.

He noted on his resume that WPI seniors dedicated their yearbook to him in 1963, in 1983, and again the year he after he retired—in 1991. Students from *Tech News* named him Man of the Year in 1967.

In his last year of full-time teaching—in 1969—he was only the second faculty member to be honored by his colleagues with the Board of Trustees' Award for Outstanding Teaching. In 1973 WPI's ROTC battalion named him an honorary colonel. WPI's Alumni Association presented him with the Robert H. Goddard Award for Outstanding Professional Achievement in 1974.

For his leadership in implementing the Plan, the Worcester Engineering Society presented him with its Scientific Achievement Award in 1979. That year he also received the Chester F. Carlson Award for educational innovation from the American Society for Engineering Education. ASEE recognized his paper on "Performance-based Engineering Education and What It Reveals" with the William Elgin Wickenden Award in 1980. ASEE's Liberal Education Division in 1988 selected him to receive what seems like the tailor-made Sterling Olmstead Award for Innovative Contributions to the Liberal Arts within Engineering Education.

IEEE named him a fellow in 1983, a distinction reserved for select individuals who have shown evidence of outstanding and extraordinary achievement in the field of electronics or computer engineering. He was cited for WPI's education program connecting technology and societal concerns. IEEE's Educational Activities Board also bestowed on Bill its Major Educational Innovation Award in 1986.

The year he retired, at WPI's 1990 Commencement Bill was awarded an honorary Doctor of Engineering degree. The trustees surprised him with their first Award for Outstanding Service, and the Department of Electrical Engineering bestowed on Bill the first Hobart Newell Award for outstanding professional accomplishments by EE alumni.

During Reunion that year, he was honored with the Teaching Excellence and Campus Leadership Award from the Sears-Roebuck Foundation, which noted "you speak many times at meetings of the faculty, a forum at which you are very much at home. Today, it is your turn to listen as we acknowledge your accomplishments as both dean and professor."

Bill received a distinctly WPI-style honor without his knowledge, although he learned about it when Jim Jackson told him at his 75th birthday celebration in 1999. After working with Bill on numerous committees, in 1987 the director of WPI's computer operations named after Bill a piece of software that generated the faculty load profile. "Using your knowledge of projects and courses, we developed a report that is still used today," Jackson told him. "I named the program after you— GROGAN_NWRPT—so every time it is run you are remembered."

It amused him to no end to tell his friends in 2006 that he had been named the winner of the William R. Grogan Award, which had been established in 1990 on the occasion of his retirement to honor extraordinary service to WPI and its students. In 2005, during the inauguration of WPI President Dennis Berkey, Bill was presented with the WPI Presidential Medal, which was inscribed, simply, "WPI Visionary."

While he never noted it on his resume, Bill was extremely honored by the dedication of the Grogan Wing in WPI's new Campus Center in 2001. He told the donor, his friend Ron Zarrella '71, that it was "the greatest thing anyone has ever done for me since my mother delivered me ... and Mae married me!" In thanking Ron, he said "this bit of immortality through the wing you had named for me is really something wonderful, and no better place for it to exist than at WPI, the home of my life's work."

Part of that work was his more than 60 years of service to his fraternity, Phi Kappa Theta, which named Bill its national Man of Achievement in August 2012.

In the last and what may have been the most meaningful award for him, Bill received the Goat's Head Award for Lifetime Commitment to WPI. His friend Bob Fitzgerald read a warm tribute to the assembled crowd at Homecoming on October 6, 2012. He recounted how in the 1950s and '60s, "everyone wanted to have Bill for an instructor because he helped students to understand engineering and use the knowledge to think creatively." The award's formal citation summed up Bill's lifelong ties to WPI. "You are as much a fixture on campus as our beloved Two Towers—a true icon of the university."

GLOBAL AMBASSADOR FOR THE PLAN

On his retirement, Bill told a reporter that "I see myself as returning to the role of teacher again, but in a different way—through writing and thinking about what we've experienced." He became a national spokesperson for innovation in engineering education. And combining two loves—the Plan and global travel—he threw himself into another role he enjoyed greatly: international ambassador for the Plan and, increasingly, unofficial quality control inspector for overseas project centers.

According to Rick Vaz '79, dean of WPI's Interdisciplinary and Global Studies Division, Bill relished advising overseas projects whenever his schedule and travel plans allowed, which kept him in touch with this increasingly important aspect of the Plan.

More often, he would visit project centers partway through the term and "play the role of 'visitor from hell,'" Vaz said. "He loved meeting students, talking about their projects, and critiquing their work."

Arriving, as Bill would say, "to inspect the troops," he would review their presentations, and the students benefitted from having a senior administrator's advice.

"Students would get all nervous," Vaz said. "He would ask very difficult questions, and then take them out for a beer and lavish them with attention."

The sudden decline in interest in engineering careers in the late 1980s caught Bill and many others in the business of technical education off guard, even though WPI's own student numbers were healthy. In reflecting on this issue, his concern extended far beyond the borders of WPI's campus. To him, this was a national crisis.

He outlined his concerns in an editorial for *Science* magazine, the publication of the American Association for the Advancement of Science, in the January 26, 1990, issue. Titled "Engineering's Silent Crisis," his essay opened with the arresting statement: "Signs of trouble in American engineering are getting little more than a shrug from government and industry, even though both have much to lose."

Bill detailed how the decline in American engineering graduates, recent MIT research that named traditionally trained engineers as a factor in the nation's lagging competitiveness, and the retirement of his generation of post-World War II engineers were contributing to a national crisis in manpower and expertise.

"Engineering schools have a clear responsibility to confront these problems head on, but they need help," he wrote. America's education system should strengthen basic language and math skills for its high school graduates. This remains a low priority as long as industry assumes that engineers from other countries will fill the country's engineering needs. Too often, companies believe that engineering tasks can be outsourced. For government and defense-related work, however, American citizenship is required. Government salaries can't compete when there is a shortage of qualified engineers. We should avoid, he argued, a "dependence born of failure to educate our own engineers."

Both industry and government need to fund scholarships for low-income students (often the first in their family to attend college and see engineering as a path to change their circumstances) and work with engineering schools to expand cooperative education and summer job programs, he said. The federal government should institute what Bill called "the equivalent of ROTC—a Reserve Engineering Training Corps (RETC)"—a selective program for high school students who, in exchange for engineering school scholarships, would serve for five years with a sponsoring government agency. The program would "ensure our government services a fresh supply of engineering talent while providing young people with both the incentive and means to pursue an engineering education."

His final question continued to sound the alarm: "Shall we continue to assume that foreign nationals will meet our engineering needs, while American youth moves to the sidelines?"

Bill's editorial raised the volume on the crisis to a dull whisper. He received a flood of letters in response and noted that many were from unemployed engineers who took offense at his description of an impending shortage. Others complained bitterly of a general tendency to undervalue engineers and their expertise, demonstrated by low federal salaries, erratic research funding, and lack of recognition for their contributions to society as a whole.

In his published response in *Science*, Bill wrote that he had predicted not a short-term shortage but a longer-term "declining presence of Americans in engineering." For him, the basic issue remained "whether industry and government consider it important that Americans continue to have a dominant role in American engineering."

The Boston Globe took up the issue in a May 1990 editorial, "Atlas is Shrugging: Engineer Shortage Looms in America." Carried widely on wire services, the column by David Warsh supported Bill's proposal for a ROTC-style program for engineering students, while acknowledging WPI's 125th anniversary year and its recent innovative approach to engineering education. The RETC idea might need "only one dedicated legislator" to push for its support, and Warsh noted several other legislative initiatives in the Senate that addressed the shortage of engineers and the lag in American science education.

"When this present-day equivalent of the Sputnik spasm comes," Warsh concluded, "let's just hope that a few good ideas come with it. ... The RETC is one that could really make a difference."

The Senate bills Warsh highlighted went nowhere, and the trouble, Bill himself concluded, was that there weren't enough engineers among the nation's policymakers who would speak to the issue with force and at a higher volume. He continued his campaign the following year, publishing "The American Engineer as Policymaker" in *Issues in Science and Technology*, published by the National Academy of Sciences.

Bill offered recommendations to shift the thinking of students already interested in leadership toward engineering, and to shift the engineering profession itself to embrace and support leadership roles. Expanding the perception of the American engineer as a decision maker in materials intended for high school students, as well as for the American public, would be initial steps to encourage people to think of engineers in policy-oriented positions as well as more traditional settings.

He broached the concept, already well-established at WPI, of broadening the training of engineers beyond a set of technical courses to acknowledge the development of human potential, and focus on communications skills, management abilities, and exposure to social and cultural fields. Encouraging undergraduates, as early as the sophomore year, to consider graduate studies, was another step to help them see pathways to a dual role as engineer and manager.

He raised his RETC program idea again to help lower-income students consider engineering as a profession, and suggested it be operated nationally through the National Science Foundation or the National Academy of Engineering. These steps in the evolution of the engineering profession would help transform the perception from nerd into knowledgeable leader.

The years of academic revolution and reform gave Bill a perspective on education that other educators wanted to learn from. From Scandinavia to southern Europe, he spent the first decade of his retirement speaking at conferences about his experiences. These speaking engagements were often combined with visits to WPI's growing list of project centers.

He was the only American educator to speak at the 1993 SEFI conference on project-organized curricula in Copenhagen. His keynote address was on project education at WPI.

"Project education has just been 'discovered' in Europe in a big way," he wrote in a trip report afterward, "and has become a major item of interest not only at the conference but also at our exchange colleges. The WPI story fascinated the audience, and I think we may be getting a few visitors shortly."

He also spoke on projects in engineering education in Espoo and Vantaa, Finland, in 1994, and on entrepreneurship and the university at the SEFI annual conference in Helsinki in 1998. Global mobility in engineering education was his topic for SEFI's meeting in Florence in 2002.

From Bill's perspective, the world continued to offer an abundance of opportunities for WPI and its students, even under a much-amended Plan. As he explained in his 1993 trip report, "Europe abounds with possibilities for WPI students and programs, especially available to them with our seven-week terms and given added flexibility with the project component, which is growing fast in Europe."

A CONTINUING REVOLUTION

At the conclusion of a two-hour orientation for new faculty members on the Plan in 1976, a member of the audience asked Romeo Moruzzi the question, "I'm wondering if you have any notion of knowing when it's time for a new revolution?"

Moruzzi's answer stands as true today for WPI as it did in that bicentennial year: "It's always time. It's going on. This is it. We're in the middle of the process. If you think that we're in the Plan now, that's wrong—it's a process."

Said Bill Shipman, "it is essential for our new faculty to realize that this revolution must be a *continuing* one and that there are logical steps and attitudes you can take to hasten it on and make it more effective in your own time."

The Plan has hastened on. On its 35th anniversary, Bill Grogan wrote, "It has often been said that the WPI Plan was 25 years ahead of its time when it was launched." In the intervening years, "not only has technology transformed in substance, but its effects upon society have been explosive."

While the Plan has proven to be an evolving organism, or as Bill said so vividly, "a live beast," its presence persists. "We at WPI have gained an enviable position through the structure of our educational program. Our challenge now lies in developing the resources and collective self-confidence to again move ahead with a new vision for the future."

CHAPTER FOUR

Life with Family and Friends

I imagine you will be lonesome for good old WPI after all. You have made some nice friends, and that place must feel like a second home.

—Irene Grogan

BILL GROGAN'S PROMISING future was securely anchored in Lee, Massachusetts. Paper and marble were the two main industries in this Western Massachusetts town, where he was born on August 2, 1924. In addition to the paper mills along the Housatonic River (one of which was among the first mills in the nation to produce paper solely from wood pulp) and a local quarry renowned for its fine marble, a host of small businesses that supported the mills and a collection of shops, schools, and churches were the small town's main employers.

Irene Grogan delivered Bill into the world 10 miles north of Lee at St. Luke's Maternity Hospital in Pittsfield, a new facility established for the growing community just six years earlier by the Roman Catholic Diocese of Springfield.

Bill's father, William Patrick Grogan, was the master machinist for the mill operated by Smith Paper Company. Bill's grandfather, Michael

Above: *Grogan's drive to achieve was clear even as a child in Lee, Massachusetts.*

Grogan, had emigrated from Ireland as a baby and married Bill's grandmother in Lee. William's job wasn't far from the family home on Laurel Street, which sat on a hill across the river from the main part of Lee. He bought the land in the summer of 1928, and working with a contractor, he built the house with $1,000 down and another $3,500 in payments made with help from a few relatives.

Life for young Billy revolved around home, school, and church. He attended St. Mary's School, the first parochial school in Berkshire County, where he was taught by the Sisters of St. Joseph. After eighth grade, he moved on to Lee High School. His family faithfully attended St. Mary's Church, where he served as an altar boy. When he was four, his sister Mary Elizabeth was born. Four years later, baby Edward joined the family. Two of his aunts, Margaret and Agnes, lived nearby and were often to be found in the Laurel Street home.

The Great Depression hit Lee's economy hard, and Bill's family had some difficult years. In an episode Bill would recount in later years as a teachable moment, he was on his way to the store one wintry day to buy food with the last of his family's funds when he was caught up in a snowball fight. The critical coin went missing and Bill, who was then no older than 12, couldn't find it anywhere in the snow. He had to trudge back up Laurel Street to confess the loss to his family. That night, they shared a can of green beans for supper.

Nothing was said at dinner, but at the end of the meal, his father gave a speech about their meager repast and emphasized the importance of taking responsibility for one's actions. Bill felt terrible, but he never forgot the lesson.

"It was very rough," said Mary Elizabeth, known as Betty to her friends, "but we had the essentials." The family would visit a farm about four miles from the house to buy dairy products, though some unpasteurized milk they bought there almost poisoned Betty and her mother once.

Their father kept a large garden and was proud to harvest a bounty of vegetables: spinach, tomatoes, cucumbers, and string beans, along with blackberries and rhubarb. Irene was "a pretty good cook," said Betty, with most dinners consisting of potatoes and vegetables along with the occasional fish, chicken, or steak. As they could, the family shared a meal with needy people who would come to the door, she recalled.

But tough times didn't seem to keep Bill down for long. As his sister was quick to say, her brother had an abundance of confidence. At St. Mary's School, "he would correct the nuns," she said, for example, when they sold "chocolate-covered graham crackers to the kids during Lent!" The nuns soon channeled his self-assurance to encourage others. Before Christmas in 1936, he gave a speech on behalf of the entire school to thank the pastor and extend holiday wishes.

"He is constantly thinking of how to make us *healthy, wealthy,* and *wise,*" intoned the young Bill Grogan. "Improvements in the school to make us *healthy,* providing means to form good habits which will make us *wealthy,* and training our souls in the ways of goodness to make us *wise;* now who can we thank for all that?"

His mother saved the typewritten speech, which included underlined words for him to emphasize, and labeled it "Billy's first speech." It stands as the first of many he would give over the next 75 years.

The budding orator also ably played the role of older brother, and was an expert in the most effective ways to tease his sister.

"I was petrified of snakes," Betty said. "And Bill would tell me there was one under my chair, or in the heating vents, and it was getting bigger." After observing one too many episodes of Bill tormenting his sister with a rubber snake, Bill's mother threw it into the furnace. He apparently came to share his sister's fear of snakes later in life, before his wartime service.

While the nuns at St. Mary's weren't always successful at reining in what Betty called Bill's "adventurous" nature, they did teach him to play the piano, and in the school's squat two-story building with its barn-like roof, they made him write with his right hand as he learned the Palmer method of penmanship. But when it came to throwing a baseball, he remained a southpaw.

Outside school, he practiced his handwriting with thank-you notes. Written carefully in pencil in cursive on wide-ruled paper, the notes Bill wrote at age six or seven to his father's sister Lucy and her husband, Bob Lewis, in Springfield, give a sense of the emerging correspondent:

> Thanks a lot for sending me and Betty those nice baskets of the Bunnies and those nice eggs. I haven't eaten any candy all during Lent and this will surely taste good to me. When are you coming up to see us?
> Love to you and Uncle Bob.
> Love, Billy

When he was eight, his understanding of Santa's travel path from east to west prompted this memo-like note just before Christmas to ask his Springfield relatives to pass along a message:

> Will you see Santa Clause [sic] for me please and have him send me the Electric train. He comes there first.
> Love, William Grogan

He grasped ideas quickly, and put his time to good use. Even in grammar school, Betty said, he kept a schedule. "He'd tell me, 'I can't go swimming, I'm scheduled to have ice cream.' It would drive me crazy."

As a kid, he had a Kodak camera and was constantly taking pictures. Betty remembers him setting up his camera and then dressing in a bandana, hat, and big overcoat to stage a jewelry box heist scene.

At Lee High School, Bill flourished. He was class president from his sophomore year on. Interested in learning about students in other countries, he was involved in a yearbook exchange with schools in Australia and England.

His page in the 1942 yearbook (which he edited) describes him as "the presiding genius of the place." Long before he entered WPI's classrooms, his nickname was "Professor" or "Doctor Grogan." Not surprisingly, he went on to coordinate many future class reunions.

And years before he would earn a patent at General Electric, his peers noted that he was "an inventor of some means," quickly adding, "although his inventions have not been put to any particular usage, they supply much comedy for onlookers." He applied his imagination by penning radio plays during his junior year, and is credited with also writing and directing a number of skits for his class.

During his senior year, Bill acquired a record player. Betty remembered that he would turn the volume up high. "He thought it was funny," she said with some exasperation, even decades later. When the record player was off, she said, he played the piano, especially the recent hit song, "Somewhere Over the Rainbow."

Good grades earned Bill the right to leave school when the *Berkshire Evening Eagle* called him to cover a story—he had become a sports stringer for the Pittsfield bureau not long after starting high school, covering high school basketball games. "Although not an athlete myself, I enjoyed the job tremendously," he wrote in a memoir. The summer before his senior year, the regular reporter was activated into the National Guard, "and I was asked if I would take his job. So, I worked out an arrangement with the school principal, which allowed me to take off in emergencies to cover stories. Along with dropout Johnny Koch, a photographer who had a car and who could pick me up, I zoomed off to cover various fires, accidents—and on one occasion—a brutal murder, which horrified my mother."

After he bought his first car, a small Ford, he was able to cover other local stories. Because the Berkshires offered a summer retreat for the country's wealthy classes, reporters from New York City would descend on the Pittsfield bureau. "These included some great journalists of the time," wrote Grogan, "like Edward R. Murrow, William L. Shirer, and Walter Lippman. I used to hang around the editorial room when they came up to file their stories, since the *Eagle* had the only teletype in the county. They would sit around for a while for coffee with the *Eagle* staff and I basked in their presence."

Career Plans Diverted

Those happy hours in the newsroom convinced Bill he was bound for a career as a reporter, and he applied to Columbia University's School of Journalism in the fall of his senior year. But world events intervened.

As he recalled in his memoir, "I was writing at our dining room table Sunday afternoon, December 7, with the NBC Symphony playing on the radio. I shall never forget what came next. 'We interrupt this program to bring you a special news bulletin: The Japanese have bombed Pearl Harbor, Hawaii, President Roosevelt has just announced.' We were at war!"

Bill and every other high school senior that year had to revise their plans. With a summer birthday, he wouldn't turn 18 until after graduation, but he was sure to be drafted soon thereafter.

Accepted into Columbia, Bill spent many evenings listening to "the fading, screeching sounds from my little short-wave radio, listening to the bulletins about the Japanese invasions of Pacific islands, and when possible, also to my beloved Edward R. Murrow from London." As he wrote, "one such evening changed my life."

His father was "superintendent of maintenance for several paper mills along the Housatonic River. One night in June, his boss, the chief engineer, Roland Packard, made a rare visit to our house. He and my father were talking in the kitchen and asked me to come downstairs. Mr. Packard was a WPI alumnus [Class of 1908], and earlier in the year had taken me down to look at Worcester Tech. I was qualified for engineering school and enjoyed the field," Bill wrote, "but I was stricken with the idea of journalism.

"Then he presented his bombshell: if I went to Columbia, I would be drafted on October 15, and he knew—he was chairman of the local draft board! But he also told me of a program called V-12 the Navy was opening at WPI and other schools which allowed students registered in engineering, science, or medicine to complete their degree on active duty."

Conducted nearly year-round, the V-12 program was a demanding academic enterprise. Failure to meet both academic and personal behavior expectations meant an automatic deployment to a Navy position.

Bill told his father he'd give it a try. He withdrew his application to Columbia and was accepted into WPI.

In the fall of 1942 (more than a decade before the construction of the

Massachusetts Turnpike), it took the family over three hours to drive from Lee, through Springfield traffic, to Worcester, where they helped move him into his room in the freshman dormitory, Sanford Riley Hall. He enlisted in the Navy on December 15.

Bill barely managed to remain at WPI. During his first term he scraped by with a C average, pulled down by poor grades in engineering drawing, chemistry, and calculus. The V-12 program got under way the following July, and it wasn't long before his "adventurous" nature confronted military discipline. Father Peter Scanlon, who later became WPI's Catholic chaplain, shared this story: listening to the radio was against naval regulations, but Bill had figured out a way to wire his room so he could listen to Worcester's local station, WTAG. He ran copper wire along the molding near the ceiling of his room, using his iron bed frame as a ground, and connected a set of earphones.

When confronted about the illegal wiring, Apprentice Seaman Grogan demonstrated his capacity for imaginative storytelling, explaining to his senior officer that he was "listening for waves from Mars." As they faded in and out, he needed to listen for the timing. The officer couldn't disprove his story, since Bill let him test the earphones in a corner of the room that had no radio reception.

Over the next year, Bill's grades improved, he joined the Catholic Theta Kappa Phi fraternity, and he began writing for the school newspaper, *Tech News*, rising eventually to the role of editor-in-chief. In the wartime V-12 program, however, he did not enjoy complete freedom of the press, especially when it came to criticizing military allies. When Bill wrote an editorial on America's eastern allies that had an anti-Russian bent, he recalled receiving "a very angry lecture from President Admiral Cluverius."

As Bill had back home, he also covered school sports for local news outlets. When the Boston bureau chief for United Press Association (forerunner of United Press International) was looking for someone to cover WPI's home football games, the Institute's public relations contact suggested Bill Grogan. After "a very commendable job indeed," Bill was recommended again, and United Press asked him to phone in his story immediately after the conclusion of WPI's game against the Coast Guard Academy.

He enjoyed receiving newsy letters from home. His mother wrote regularly with family updates and details about his friends' wartime action, the Red Cross collections, and the soap and cigarette shortages that marked life on the home front. He must have sent his laundry back to Lee, as in one letter from June 1944, Irene Grogan reported, "I sent back your entire laundry case as the towel wasn't dried yet. This has been a terrible week for the wash. Having no heat in the house makes it worse." Recognizing the effort his studies required, particularly in electrical engineering, she closed her letter, "Will be praying for you dear, that exam of EE will come out alright."

After three years of nearly continuous classes, with only brief leaves between terms, Bill prepared to graduate from WPI in June 1945, just over a month after the end of the war in Europe. His mother thought he might be getting a little nostalgic. Her comments were prescient: "I imagine you will be lonesome for good old WPI after all," she wrote. "You have made some nice friends, and that place must feel like a second home."

Arrangements for his family to attend Commencement triggered a flurry of calls and letters about buses, trains, and shared rides from Springfield. They formed a proud audience for the ceremony, where Bill read the class history, which covered just 999 days. His academic record had more than improved; he received his bachelor of science in electrical engineering with distinction, and won the Salisbury Prize for completing his requirements "faithfully, industriously, and with distinguished attainment." In addition to his election to two national honor societies, Tau Beta Pi (for engineering) and Sigma Xi (for research), he was also named permanent class historian. As the *Berkshire Eagle* reported, he was selected for inclusion in *Who's Who in American Colleges and Universities.*

When the Navy's orders finally came, less than three weeks before Commencement, he learned he'd be heading to Columbia University after all, not as a journalism student, but as an assistant seaman in the

U.S. Naval Reserve Midshipman School. While his training continued, the war wound toward its conclusion with the Japanese surrender that August.

While Bill served the post-war Navy in several capacities with distinction (see Chapter 5), he was discharged and back on campus within a year. He remained a loyal member of the Class of 1946, and, as class historian, was able to participate in Commencement exercises that June when the last remaining members of his class received their degrees. He returned to stay in September 1946 as an instructor in electrical engineering while he worked toward a master's degree, which he received in 1949.

Family life went on back in Lee. Betty graduated from high school in 1946 and worked as a switchboard operator for New England Telephone. She met Thomas McNamara through work and they became engaged in March 1950. Ed excelled in his high school studies, and was accepted to attend Holy Cross in Worcester for the fall of 1950.

Bill's father continued as foreman of the machine shop at Smith Paper. The postwar economy meant more pressures for productivity, but no additional pay, which led to strikes or, from William Grogan's perspective, just general resentment. In a letter sent to Bill in early 1946, he wrote, "No Bill, I did not get any raise but I got two more engineers over me to see if I can't get out more work…. There has been quite a lot of colds and sickness up here. The G.E. in Pittsfield are out on strike, we are just as busy but the condenser may fall off if it keeps up."

The stress took its toll. In September 1950, Bill's father suffered a fatal heart attack at age 61, just three months after Betty and Thomas's wedding and Ed's high school graduation.

The senior Grogan's death challenged the family in several ways, most immediately for Ed, who came home to support his mother while he worked in a General Electric laboratory in Pittsfield. With assistance from Bill, now an assistant professor at WPI, Ed eventually returned to classes at Holy Cross, graduating in 1956 with a chemistry degree and a commission as an ensign in the Naval Reserve. That same year, Irene moved to Worcester to live with Bill, who was in the process of purchasing a new home near the WPI campus on Laconia Road. Ed returned from active duty to Lee and lived in the Laurel Street home for several years. Irene passed away in Worcester on October 16, 1960.

LIFE BEYOND WPI

While Bill Grogan would spend the rest of his days living within a short drive of campus, he built an active life beyond WPI that involved travel, friends, and church. He joined the Rotary Club of Worcester in 1955 and only stepped back from those volunteer activities in 1972 after his administrative work took much more of his time.

His faith had always been a central part of his life, and in Lee, St. Mary's Church served as a social center for his family. He kept among his papers a printed message that had been pinned on the wall at Laurel Street for years. Titled "Consecration of the Family to the Sacred Heart," the prayer asked Jesus for blessings on the family in exchange for the consecration of "the trials and the joys and all the happiness of our family life." All five family members signed their names in ink. The prayer was dated December 6, 1941, one day before the Japanese attack on American forces at Pearl Harbor.

At WPI, Bill joined the Newman Club for Catholic students, rising to become its president, and pledged to Theta Kappa Phi. When he was recalled to military service from 1951 to 1952, during the Korean War, his deployment took him to Rome, where he had not one but two audiences with Pope Pius XII. He sent a medal blessed by the pontiff to a Franciscan cleric and friend, Brother Cairnan.

In the note he received in reply, the Franciscan noted that from the tone of Bill's letter, "the Catholic boys on the *Stoddard* and her sister ship are making a fine showing for God and country." He ended by praising "the good example you give to others ... you certainly are doing Catholic Action of the highest type and are certainly to be encouraged."

Bill shared the news about his visits with the Pope with many people. In her response to the letter he wrote her, his mother praised his storytelling skills:

Received your wonderful letter and cards, telling of your trip to Rome and the audience with the Pope. From your description dear, it must have been out of this world. In reading your wonderful letter, I felt as if I was right there and could almost picture everything about what it must be in my mind. Billy you certainly write a beautiful story.

Back home in Worcester, he faithfully attended Mass each week at his local church, Immaculate Conception. He helped raise money for the pastoral center named for the famed military chaplain Father Ed Connors. It was an expansive one-story structure built on the hill behind the church.

"Bill was a tremendous Catholic," said Father Scanlon, who met Grogan in 1961 when the priest returned to Worcester as associate pastor at Immaculate Conception, charged to work with college students. Scanlon became a member of and an advisor to Bill's fraternity and in 1969 was named WPI's Catholic chaplain on a full-time basis. That year, the Diocese of Worcester appointed Bill to a committee to assess its educational programs. Two years later, he joined the Diocesan Board of Education, which he chaired from 1974 to 1976 and served again from 1993 to 1997.

MEETING MAE AND SETTLING DOWN

The church was a natural source for social connection for Bill, who found friendships as well as spiritual solace from his fellow parishioners. So when his friends wanted to introduce him to a young widow, a devout Catholic with a flair for interior design, a church wedding seemed an appropriate setting.

The first time Bill met Mae Jeanne Kafer, she was an autumn vision, petite in a pumpkin-tinted bridesmaid's dress. The occasion was the wedding of Connie Deleon and Pete Ottowitz '58 in Garden City, Long Island. Held on October 7, 1961, the event included happy family and friends from Skidmore and WPI, and Ottowitz's WPI fraternity brothers from Theta Kappa Phi. His twin sister Joan was the maid of honor, and the best man was his friend and professor, Bill Grogan.

A Brooklyn native and a graduate of Erasmus Hall High School and the Traphagen School of Design, Mae was an interior designer by training. Her career, however, had taken her to Chase Manhattan Bank and then to Riegel Paper Corporation's headquarters in Manhattan, where she was an executive assistant. In 1950 she had married Connie's cousin, Ted Sperl. But she was now a young widow after Ted's untimely death, in 1959, from a cerebral hemorrhage at the age of 33.

As far as Mae's relatives were concerned, a family wedding offered an easy way for her to meet eligible partners. And Bill's friends knew his sociable nature kept him busy. He had enjoyed friendships with other women, but no one had yet captured his heart.

After the Garden City ceremony, the families and friends drove into Manhattan for a reception at the tony New York Athletic Club. As the bride and groom prepared to leave the festivities, the wedding party accompanied them the few blocks to the Pan Am building at the foot of Park Avenue. They all went to the rooftop for what they thought would be a once-in-a-lifetime sendoff. There, a helicopter waited to fly the newlyweds to the airport to begin their honeymoon.

The happy couple wanted their friends to share their wedded happiness. "We were hoping that Mae and Bill would connect," said Connie. "But they didn't start dating right away." Between 1962 and 1965, Bill spent a lot of time consulting with the Navy on several torpedo projects. On his travels back and forth to Washington, D.C., he managed to stop in New York and see Mae. Over time, she ventured north to New England with him, and the couple would stay overnight with the Ottowitzes (in separate rooms).

"I felt funny chaperoning my professor," said Ottowitz with a smile.

In a datebook carefully preserved from 1965, Bill recorded his visits to New York and Mae's trips to Lee to see his family and attend a few Boston Pops concerts at Tanglewood. On November 17, he wrote out his plan in capital letters: "PROPOSE TO MAE." But a request from Washington must have changed his timing, as the 17th is circled with an arrow moving it up to November 10. He spent two separate weekends in December in New York City, most likely making plans for the wedding, to be scheduled as soon as the couple could manage all the details.

They were married in heart of midtown, in the Lady Chapel of St. Patrick's Cathedral, right across Fifth Avenue from Rockefeller Center. It was January 29, 1966. Connie Ottowitz was the maid of honor, decked out in a deep fuchsia gown with short sleeves, as she recalled.

"It was snowy," she said. "We were freezing." Bill's brother Ed was the best man, and Pete Ottowitz was an usher.

After their reception at the New York Athletic Club, the couple headed to Puerto Rico and the Virgin Islands for their 10-day honeymoon—and just as their friends had done, they rode in a helicopter from the Pan Am building to the airport to make their flight. They held a second reception later for their New England friends at one of Bill's favorite places, the Old Mill Restaurant in Westminster.

The honeymoon would be the first of many trips together for the couple. Bill's years at sea with the Navy had fed his fascination for traveling and new experiences. The couple headed to the Caribbean at some point every winter, but over time their itineraries grew more complex.

To underwrite his taste for travel, Bill joined an investment club, known as the Boynton Associates, in the early 1960s. He became a devoted reader of the *Wall Street Journal*. He often hosted the club's monthly meetings, where the members reviewed the stocks and voted whether to buy or sell, working with a local broker. The group's half-dozen or so members were drawn from WPI faculty and staff.

"We'd invest as a group," explained retired civil engineering professor Frank DeFalco '58. "No wild speculation. We each put in a weekly amount. No big winners, just nice and steady. It was fun socially—we'd have snacks and drinks." After 20 or 25 years, he said, several members moved out of the area, and the group voted to sell everything and split the proceeds. Bill's interest in personal finance eventually led to his service as a trustee of Worcester's independent community bank, Bay State Savings Bank, for more than 25 years.

One long-planned vacation had to adjust its itinerary when the faculty vote on the WPI Plan came sooner than expected. Only a few days after that fateful vote, the couple left for Europe via Iceland, where friend and fraternity brother Jack Bresnahan '68 was stationed with the Navy. It was Mae's first trip to Europe.

That June she recorded her thoughts and impressions. Largely commenting on the food ("yummy"), transportation ("Trains are great. *So glad* we have Eurail pass!"), and the views ("most magnificent"), she admired tea served in glasses with holders, noted the effect of feather pillows on her hay fever, and chronicled a night at Bill's favorite beer hall in Stuttgart. Near the end of her diary, she offered this poetic summary of their nearly three-week journey:

Large tubs
Large towels
Small spoons
Small forks
Small trays
Flowers always (achoo)...
Whistles, chimes
Bells, showers!

Mae delighted in the European personalities they met, and loved the fact that, six years after their mid-life wedding, visitors in one Swiss mountainside tea spot mistook them for honeymooners.

Bill was devoted to her, and his friends agreed she had a calming effect on him. They regularly attended Mass together at Immaculate Conception. Father Scanlon, then the associate priest, warmly recalled the Ash Wednesday afternoon service held after their wedding. Mae came down the aisle on crutches.

"Suddenly Bill appears behind her," he said. "As she approaches the altar rail, Bill cuts in front of her and introduces me to his wife, Mae." He quickly explained to the priest that on her first day back in Worcester after the honeymoon, she had slipped on the ice and injured her ankle. It was not her ideal introduction to the congregation, Bill said later. According to Father Pete Scanlon, "he was afraid that the people in church might have come to the conclusion that he was a wife beater."

A few years after the wedding, Mae's parents, Herb and Mae Kafer, left Brooklyn and moved to Worcester: first to an apartment, and when they needed more care, into the house on Laconia Road. Built as a cozy two-bedroom, Bill and Mae's home had only one full bathroom. Sharing the facilities proved challenging, as more than once, someone would have to pound on the door to encourage the occupant to hurry up.

LIFE ON LACONIA ROAD

It wasn't long before Bill decided to add a master bedroom and bath to the back of the house. He and Mae moved into the new addition and the two couples shared the living room, dining room, and kitchen. The arrangement seemed to work for everyone. Mae's mother passed away in November 1983; her father died in April 1986.

Ten Laconia Road remained a central location for fun and friendship. Mae transformed the former bachelor pad (the moose antlers came off the mantel) into a tastefully decorated home that was warm and welcoming. The genial host continued to entertain fraternity students, visiting trustees, and, as the Plan emerged, committee members primed to map out WPI's future over three-minute steaks and scotch. Mae was a good sport, ready with hors d'oeuvres, a sense of humor, and a good meal.

When conversation turned to WPI business "at dinner, she would excuse herself and disappear," Jack Bresnahan recalled. He and his wife, Kathy, lived in the neighborhood when their four children were small, and they all spent time at the Grogan house. Mae was the children's surrogate grandmother, baking cookies and walking with them to Indian Lake. Bill served as an occasional Santa Claus, and he and Mae were godparents to the Bresnahans' youngest son, Matt.

On cold wintry days in Worcester, the happy couple often showed their friends slides of their Caribbean travels, accompanied by recordings of steel drums and other tropical tunes. If the scenes were of Europe, Bill would find appropriate classical music or German marching bands for his soundtrack. He would describe the history of their destinations to the delight of his audiences. "It was the opposite of a snoozy slide show," his sister Betty recalled.

The couple's passports were filled with stamps from trips every year. "Bill often told me his one weakness was travel," said Jack Bresnahan.

Not included in the slide shows from a 1972 trip to Europe were Grogan's three visits to Swiss dentists to cope with a toothache. Fortunately, fellow WPI faculty member Willy Eggimann could make a local recommendation. After Bill's $43 root canal "and lots of colorful stories!" wrote Mae in her diary, "we went to tea to relieve our tensions! Yummy!"

The couple enjoyed nearly 25 years of married bliss. "Bill's world revolved around her," observed Connie Ottowitz. "It was a real love affair."

"It was clear they adored each other," agreed his faculty colleague John Orr.

Mae enjoyed writing poetry, and in 1987 Bill had a set of her poems printed in a small pamphlet.

Losing Mae, and Almost Himself

Mae had always been petite, standing just over five feet tall and weighing less than 90 pounds. "We used to joke that Mae's weight was in ounces, not pounds," said fraternity trustee Nick Scalera. "They were the unlikely couple."

"A little bird lady," is how Mary-Louise Eggimann described her. "She always looked fragile, but mentally, she was very strong." The only time she would get angry, she said, was when Bill would have too much to drink. She knew how to calm him down when his emotions would get the best of him.

She became frail as her health declined in the 1980s. "You could tell by how he walked into the office how Mae was," recalled Doris Horgan, executive assistant to dean of faculty Ray Bolz, Bill's next door neighbor in Boynton Hall.

While the stories of her health challenges varied among their friends, at one point Mae may have contracted hepatitis from contaminated dental instruments. She was prone to infections, and took steroids to combat her illness. An unfortunate side effect, however, was a noticeably hunched posture in her later years.

According to Bill's friend Carol Garofoli, a summer spider bite in 1990 proved too much for her system to overcome. She ended up in St. Vincent's Hospital, seemed to rally, and then after a few days, succumbed to the infection and died. It was September 8, the Saturday after Labor Day.

Bill was devastated. Retired for only three months, he had planned many trips with Mae. In his mind, he would be making up for all that time he'd spent serving WPI instead of spending time with her. It would be a month before he could leave the house.

His friends and fraternity brothers set up a rotation schedule so they could be with him around the clock. He spent his first Christmas without Mae at the Bresnahans' home near Hamilton, Canada. Ron Zarrella '71 took him fishing in Canada. But even good friends can't keep up a minding schedule forever. In the months after her death, his neighbors kept him company on the weekends. "Sundays were hard for him," said a neighbor. His wife who had been raised in the house across the street from Bill, said "We would hear him … oh, it was sad. He wailed in the house."

Trying to function better in the outside world, Bill turned to alcohol. Always a social drinker, having grown up in a society that saw alcohol as a social lubricant, he had remained in control, or so it seemed to most people. But after Mae's death, he became less coherent in his conversations with friends. Those who worked closely with him found he was at his best only before noon. A group gathered to express their concern that the person they knew and loved had changed his behavior, and they feared the worst. Drastic steps were needed.

Together, they planned an intervention—a carefully scripted encounter with someone suffering from an addiction—to persuade him to enter a rehabilitation facility. They held a rehearsal beforehand.

On the chosen day, Bill was invited to come to the WPI president's house. He thought he would be meeting with interim president and

WPI classmate John Lott Brown '46. But Brown wasn't home. Instead, eight of his close friends—fellow faculty members, WPI colleagues, a fraternity brother, and a family member—greeted him as he entered. Each read to him a brief account of how his behavior had affected them.

"He was hurt," recalled Denise Rodino, a senior member of the development office who had also lost a spouse and had helped Bill through some of his grieving process. "He didn't believe people noticed his drinking."

While Bill thanked them and said he would take their advice under consideration, one friend was at Laconia Road pulling together some of his clothes. Eventually, he agreed to be driven to a facility in Vermont.

Eight or ten days later, Jim Demetry got the call to bring him home. "We had a long talk on the drive back," he said. Bill's stay in Vermont wasn't long enough. Most programs require at least 28 days to help alcoholics change their drinking habits and find new coping skills. He had attended Alcoholics Anonymous meetings while he was there.

But the power of his friends' concern had an impact. As Rodino said, "it changed his drinking to more acceptable levels." Carol Garofoli would accompany him to WPI events, and they agreed he would stick to glasses of Coke in public. He also realized he shouldn't drive and endanger others, which several friends had noted during the intervention.

Most likely as a way to learn more about the field of addiction treatment, Bill joined the board of directors for Spectrum Addiction Services for a four-year term from 1992 to 1996.

He later described to his advisee and housemate Sean Donohue '93 one therapeutic treatment that did help him cope with his grief. Bill had a timeshare at the Trapp Family Lodge in Stowe, Vermont, and spent several weeks there each year. As he had approached retirement, he and Mae had picked out a plot to build a vacation home in the area.

After Mae's death, "he was grieving really hard," said Donohue. "He had a hard time sleeping, working, even thinking." Bill met a massage therapist in Stowe, who said her technique would help release all his pent-up emotion.

"She warned him," Donohue said. She cautioned the widower that he would experience "an overwhelming release of emotion." As Bill told Donohue, during the massage he "bawled like a baby for an hour." But from that point on, he was able to accept Mae's death, although he would never entirely get over it.

The house felt less empty once Bill decided to take in boarders. His new housemates were typically graduate students in need of temporary housing, and they were often the recipients of unsolicited advice. Donohue, who had remained Bill's advisee, despite changing majors from EE to civil engineering, was one of the first. He recalled cleaning out the basement in the fall of 1993 to create room for a bed and a place to study.

As they worked together in the basement, Bill found a pair of green slippers that Mae had been looking for. "We shared a moment," said Donohue. "He was always talking about her." He had met her in the fall of 1989 when he first visited their home as a freshman advisee. "The two of them were so awesome together," he remembered. "You could feel the amount of love they had for each other, how they treated each other, spoke to each other."

In the spring of 1996, Martin Bertogg came to live at 10 Laconia Road. A Swiss exchange student from ETH, the Swiss Federal Institute of Technology, he had arrived in Worcester to study structural engineering. Bob Fitzgerald had encouraged him to change his focus to fire protection engineering, which meant he would need to stay in Worcester longer to finish his studies. Bertogg met Bill through EE professor Willy Eggimann at a dinner party in the winter of 1995, and Bill offered him the room recently vacated by Donohue.

"For me, it was an opportunity for housing, but for Bill it was a chance for company," Bertogg recalled. His "rent" was the requirement that he mow Bill's lawn every two weeks. "And it was not a big lawn," he added. While his time on Laconia Road was "a short part of my life," Bertogg said, "it was very inspirational."

He rarely had to cook a meal. He either enjoyed some of Bill's famous three-minute steaks or they explored new restaurants around Worcester together. Bill also enjoyed homemade fondue, perhaps with some advice from his Swiss boarder, and he took pride in his different dipping sauces. "I was somebody good to have around for conversation," Bertogg said. What continually impressed him, he said, was Bill's vigor. Five years after his official retirement, he was still advising students every day.

"He was very future-oriented," said Bertogg, "not dwelling in the past." This gave him the energy to try new things, he said. Grogan's ability to embrace new technology also impressed him, as older people in continental Europe were less interested in trying new things.

AROUND THE WORLD WITH BILL

Throughout the 1990s and early 2000s, Bill Grogan also embraced the world. The trips he'd planned to take with Mae turned into journeys with friends and companions. As his nephew, Tom McNamara, reminded Bill's friends in his eulogy, "Bill would say, the only trip he regrets is the one he did not take." His refrigerator, filled with condiments from Europe, was typically covered with magnets from far-flung places.

While some travels involved visits to WPI project centers, more frequently they were just for fun. "He loved to design trips," said Lance Schachterle, professor of literature and former associate provost for academic affairs. "He'd do all the legwork, he made all the arrangements." And if a conference took them to an unusual location, such as Helsinki, Bill would add on a special twist. After a meeting on international engineering education in September 2000, he and Lance spent three days in St. Petersburg, with a side trip flying 400 miles up to the Arctic Circle to see wild reindeer in Lapland's Santa Claus Village.

Mae's cousin, Terry Quinn, was a frequent traveling companion. Her niece noted that Terry kept a suitcase packed with matching outfits ready to go in case Bill called. George and Marilyn Saltus spent time on many sunny beaches with Bill, including "his favorite places in the world," St. John in the U.S. Virgin Islands, Aruba, and Hawaii for Thanksgiving, when there were fewer crowds along the Kona coast. "He loved snorkeling," Saltus said, and they would track the fish they had spotted.

On the other end of the temperature scale, he spent several Christmases in Quebec City with Terry and other friends at the Chateau Frontenac. No matter where he traveled, Bill faithfully sent a postcard to Carol Garofoli. Her collection documents his post-retirement global explorations, from Vermont to Australia's Great Barrier Reef.

"He kept going full tilt," said his advisee and friend Rick Vaz, comparing Bill to a cartoon character that leans forward so far "that he has to keep moving his feet to keep from falling face first. He charged around the world as regularly and often as he could. Taking cruises. All sorts of wonderful exotic travel, as long as he possibly could. Because he loved seeing the world, and it's remarkable how long he was able to do it."

After fraternity brother Pete Miraglia graduated from WPI in 1995, he and Bill took a trip together every year until Miraglia's wedding in 2005. No matter their destination, Bill would bring up Mae in the conversation. "She was always on his mind," he said. When Miraglia completed his PhD program in materials science, his advisor's graduation gift to him was a four-week trip around the world. From Boston to Tahiti, to Sydney, Bangkok, Beijing, and Italy, they logged 52,860 miles together. Despite a 50-year difference in age, theirs was a strong friendship. "No one could figure it out," Miraglia said, "but he was always there for me."

"He valued his friends so much," he recalled. "He always tried to keep in touch, almost to a fault. He'd send news clippings, emails … make calls. You knew he really cared."

To many people, WPI, its faculty, staff, and students, seemed like Bill's extended family. Off campus and beyond the academic calendar, his friends and neighbors knew him in what they called "real time." Although they weren't as close by, from his family's perspective, Betty said, he wasn't "the dean," he wasn't "the professor," "he was just Bill— never high and mighty. He drove an old car, had a small house, was very humble. He clipped coupons, but enjoyed the best—fine dining and, very important to him, atmosphere."

From an early age, Bill Grogan had a way of creating an environment that encouraged connections, fostered friendships, and found some fun along the way.

CHAPTER FIVE

A Better Citizen and a Better Patriot

My service in the Navy was my IQP.

—Bill Grogan

BILL GROGAN'S CHOICE of college was a military decision. In the spring of 1942, his selection of WPI over Columbia University's journalism program reflected his clear-eyed recognition of the nation's wartime status. It was a decision that would change the course of his life.

Attending WPI, where a Navy V-12 college training unit would soon be formed, would provide a path toward officer status, as well as a certain level of control over his destiny during the war. After the attack on Pearl Harbor halfway through his senior year in high school, nearly all 18-year-old American males faced the draft. Bill would turn 18 in August 1942, and he recognized that if he enrolled at Columbia, he would be drafted into the Army within a few months.

And in the Navy, he reasoned, he'd encounter fewer snakes. While his sister insists he tormented her with a replica as a child, he recalls developing a serious, lifelong case of ophidiophobia after a pre-school

Above: *Grogan reports to Midshipman School in New York in the summer of 1945.*

encounter with a large specimen slithering through the woods behind the family house.

The United States established V-12 programs at 131 schools across the country to significantly bolster the ranks of military officers. WPI was one of those selected to participate in the Navy's V-12 program, and by 1943 the Institute had faculty and housing in place to accommodate the anticipated influx of students. Bringing the military to WPI seemed natural enough. At the outbreak of World War II, WPI's president was a U.S. Navy rear admiral, Wat Tyler Cluverius, who had succeeded the late Ralph Earle, another rear admiral and classmate of Cluverius at the U.S. Naval Academy.

The program proved beneficial for the school's ongoing health and stability. Grogan's incoming Class of 1946—209 men—arrived on campus in September 1942, but "draft notices flew like the snowflakes of that especially harsh winter," Bill later wrote, and just 148 were left by spring. A welcome influx of students arrived when the school's V-12 unit officially began on July 1, 1943. Their numbers enabled WPI to retain faculty members, who in turn supported broader course offerings, and to keep student athletics, fraternities, and other organizations relatively intact. Before the end of his junior year, however, 75 percent of the original members of Bill's class were no longer at WPI.

The Class of 1946 had something of a schizophrenic history, starting off as a group of freshmen enjoying typical college experiences, but soon morphing into a band of cadets enduring military training. At that time, all freshmen were housed in Sanford Riley Hall (WPI's only dormitory), where they engaged in the usual hijinks of those days: water bags dropped down four flights of stairs, sophomore hazing involving shredded pants and unsolicited haircuts, the school-sanctioned Paddle Rush (a free-for-all that sprawled across the football field), and the Rope Pull (with the losers splashing into Institute Pond).

But soon the campus took on the more serious atmosphere of what Lt. Cdr. Albert J. Schwieger, assistant commanding officer of the WPI unit throughout the V-12 program, called "a partially autonomous Navy organization, almost as big as the civilian college." Quickly, the rowdiness faded away as the daily routine became "work-eat-sleep-work," as the WPI Class of 1946 yearbook recounted. Even physical education classes took on a military tone, and the physical education teacher, Chief Petty Officer Charles "Mac" McNulty, became famous for his "Commando Course." As the population of cadets increased, Stratton Hall was converted into additional dormitory space.

A Little More Education

After graduating from the accelerated program at WPI in June 1945, Bill Grogan left Worcester for two weeks' leave in Lee. Just a few weeks earlier, he had learned he would be assigned to the U.S. Naval Reserve Midshipman School at Columbia University, starting July 9. While it wasn't journalism school, it also wasn't an express trip to the Pacific Theater, where the war continued to rage.

Relieved at the news, he telephoned his family, as his mother noted in a June 8 letter. "It was good to hear your voice yesterday," she wrote. "I think, dear, maybe everything is for the best. That it turned out Columbia. I just received your letter explaining everything about it. As long, Bill, as you can keep going to school, and keeping out of it, and also a little more education is something."

Most of his fellow WPI classmates would join him in New York City. Columbia had converted a dozen buildings to house the training center and the seamen. A parallel program, housing hundreds more, ran on the USS *Prairie State*, anchored at a nearby dock. Halfway through the training, the ship residents traded places with the dormitory occupants, and each group had a new environment to keep shipshape under the watchful eyes of the drill masters. Columbia's program had grown to be the largest in the country, with about 9,000 graduates a year. Grogan's was a class of 1,349 men, close to 85 percent of them engineers from schools across the country. They were the 26th and final group to complete the program there.

After a one-month indoctrination period, which involved many carefully scrutinized personal and room inspections, formations, drills, and reviews, Bill became a midshipman. His first two weeks' pay came to $5, after deductions for uniforms and laundry. Then came another 90 days of midshipman school (known as the V-7 program), with classes and practical training in ordnance, navigation, damage control, and seamanship. In a flexible adjustment to their coursework, after the Japanese surrender on August 15 ended the war, classes on the identification of airplane and naval vessel types were replaced by lessons in naval law. Outside the classroom, Bill served as a staff member for the final issue of the school's yearbook, *Side Boy*.

WINNING THE PEACE

His coursework at Columbia continued through October 1945. The final graduation for the Midshipman School was held November 2 at the Cathedral of St. John the Divine. Although still under construction (as it had been for the previous 100 years), it was an edifice large enough to accommodate the 1,121 graduates, who received their commissions from Secretary of the Navy James Forrestal, witnessed by some 5,000 well-wishers. Midshipman Grogan, now an ensign in the U.S. Naval Reserve, was placed on active status.

His entire class had been told soon after the war's end that most would be able to return to civilian life after graduation, but by the end of September, the Navy reversed course on demobilization and instead planned sea duty assignments for nearly all the newly commissioned officers. As the school's leader, Commodore John Richards, explained at graduation, "The peace has not yet been won," and the reservists' peacetime responsibilities were no less great than "in the terrible crisis just past."

Secretary Forrestal expanded on this theme in his remarks. "You are accepting commissions when the fighting is finished, but the need for the services of men such as yourselves still exists," he said. "The job of the United States Navy is not finished. It will not be, either in your lifetime or mine, because no matter how deep our faith in the construction of the world society built on law, power, and force, both moral and physical, it will nevertheless be necessary to that new order if it is to have a practical chance of working."

Bill received a welcome 10-day post-graduation leave, which he spent in Lee with his family. He reported for duty at the Brooklyn Navy Yard, but by January 1946 he had traveled across the country by train, transferred to the U.S. Naval Electronics Laboratory in San Diego. There, according to his longtime friend George Saltus, Bill spent time translating instruction manuals from captured German destroyers to learn how their electronic equipment operated. The laboratory was housed on the USS *Marysville*, a patrol craft rescue escort ship (PCER 857). Every once in a while, he noted in a letter to his family, he sailed aloft in a blimp for reconnaissance training. He disliked the rough rides, he said.

To extend the ensigns' training, the laboratory sailed out to sea as one of the Navy's Underway Training Units. Bill was being trained as an electronics specialist, but like everyone else in his unit, he also had to learn routine and emergency shipboard operations. "Shipriders," also called "Inspector-Instructors," observed everything and these specially trained officers and enlisted men stood ready to issue corrections or improvements aimed at making standard procedures more efficient.

The Navy completed its demobilization by September 1, 1946, and the newly promoted Lieutenant (junior grade) Grogan was free to return to civilian life for the first time since 1942. He headed back to WPI for graduate work in electrical engineering, earning a master's degree in 1949 while also serving as an instructor. His reserve status meant the Navy was never far away, however. In fact, he spent part of the summer before his last year of graduate school on reserve duty in Havana. After earning his master's degree, he was appointed an assistant professor and taught full-time in the EE department for the next two years.

RECALLED

When the Korean conflict heated up in 1951, the Navy recalled Bill for 24 months, starting on February 15. He had hoped that as an engineer his assignment would be land-based, but instead he learned that he

121

would be going out to sea again, this time on a destroyer. He appealed to WPI's president (and Navy man) to see whether he could pull any strings to change his assignment.

As Bill told the story in later years, he knew right away that his chances for reassignment were nil when President Cluverius, hearing his request, responded with a jovial, "Destroyers: backbone of the Navy!"

His department head, Theodore Morgan, knew Bill would be hard to replace midyear, so he also appealed to Cluverius, hoping he could engineer a delay in Bill's assignment. As "his services are particularly needed in the EE Department for the coming term," he wrote, "due to the constantly increasing demand for electrical engineers, it would be practically impossible to obtain a replacement for Professor Grogan at the middle of the college year. Consequently, a request for further delay would appear to be fully justified."

Morgan's request was also denied. Bill reported for duty in mid-February 1951, as required by his country. He was assigned to the USS *Stoddard* (DD-566), a destroyer that had been retired after its service during World War II and then pulled out of mothballs for this new conflict (later serving with distinction during the Vietnam War). The ship spent time in the Charleston Naval Shipyard in South Carolina before the March 9 recommissioning, then continued south to the Caribbean, with Lt. Grogan aboard as electronics officer.

Bill served under Commander Eli T. Reich for the next 13 months, while the *Stoddard* completed shakedown cruises along the East Coast and down to Guantanamo Bay, Cuba. Command did not always go smoothly for Capt. Reich, and Bill may have been the cause of a few wrinkles in his command. An enigmatic bill for five dollars to cover the cost of a broken swimming pool door from the Officers' Mess at Guantanamo Bay, addressed to Lt. (j.g.) W. R. Grogan, suggests a military story that Bill may not have shared as widely as some others.

After the Caribbean cruises, Commander Reich was replaced in 1952, just before the *Stoddard* sailed for Europe. Bill shed some light on Reich's management style in a letter to his mother in April 1952, just a few days into the ship's Atlantic crossing.

In comparison with Reich, he wrote:

> The new Captain seems OK. He is very quiet, but seems to know his job well, and is certainly a lot calmer than Capt. Reich. It is a little early to tell yet, but it seems like he will be very easy to get along with. We certainly have had some tremendous problems come up in the past few days, and he has been very calm about the whole thing. We seem to have gone off without some very important instructions, and he just waited until we could transfer them from another ship. Capt. Reich would have gone out of his mind if it happened with him.

Touchy temper aside, Reich recognized Grogan's talents. Within two months of arriving on board ship, Bill passed an exam and was selected as a member of the cryptoboard, authorized to encrypt messages and handle classified information. In August, he completed a three-week course on anti-submarine warfare in Key West, Florida.

By late October 1951, Reich supported Bill's bid to change his designation from a line billet to a special billet for electronics. In his endorsement, he wrote that his electronics officer's performance of his technical duties with electronics installations was "eminently satisfactory," and "elevated the general technical knowledge of the officers and men who have been associated with him." Reich continued that Bill "possesses officer-like qualities to a high degree. It is believed his very wide educational background in electronics and his keen interest in engineering matters can be advantageously used by the Navy."

It would have been a rare exception for the Navy to grant Bill's request, and, in fact, it did not. The Navy's response noted that "the most pressing need continues to be for junior line officers to fill general service billets at sea." While he may have had significant civilian qualifications, the determination was largely based on his naval qualifications. The letter closed with the assurance that should the Navy's requirements and Grogan's ambitions happen to intersect, "Your special qualifications and preference for next duty assignment … will be given every consideration consistent with the needs of the Service in determining your next duty assignment."

ELECTRONICS AND OPERATIONS

Even without the desired change in his designation, Bill continued to serve as an electronics officer and operations officer for the USS *Stoddard*. He pursued additional training as he could, including four weeks in Combat Information Center school in Boston around Thanksgiving.

The crew became accustomed to the ship during its first cruise to the Caribbean. The *Stoddard* was stationed in Guantanamo, but visited other islands, including Jamaica for what Bill described as "quite a week-end" in June 1951. In vivid detail, he shared the story of his Jamaican adventures in one of the many typed letters he sent to his mother back in Lee.

> We got there about 0500 Saturday morning, and liberty began about 7. A group of officers, including myself, and also a few chiefs and men immediately took off. Kingston is reputed to be a terrible place. … From people on other ships we had heard about this place on the north side of the Island called the Tower Island Hotel … decided to make a week-end of it, and hired a big touring car, and drove 60 miles across some very rugged mountains over a winding narrow road (which I can only describe with my hands when I return), and arrived at Tower Isle. … We had a wonderful time there—it was such a change from the ship. It seems it is now off season for them, and they have much reduced prices. I guess during the winter, rooms average about $60–70 a day. We got them for $11/day, which includes 4 excellent meals, which is very reasonable. Of course the rate of exchanges helps tremendously, too.
>
> It was certainly a dream place. … We took it easy, swam, sat in the sun, and watched all the performers they have—"callipso [sic] singers" they call them. I could have stayed there about a week, and might regain some lost youth these past rugged months have cost.
>
> But as all things must end, so did this, and we left Sunday about 10, getting back in time for the last mass at the cathedral in Kingston. I had the duty from mid-afternoon until we sailed (which was about 7).

That was also fantastic, exciting, but not too pleasant. The pier was lined with hawkers selling all sorts of stuff, and the sailors were continually leaning over the rail dealing with them. Some of them tried to climb aboard, and I had my hands full keeping them off with the aid of about 4 dock sentries, four gangway sentries, and three topside sentries. The topside sentries had M-1 rifles, I had a .45 (but no bullets—just for effect). Our biggest peace-keeping device was the fire hose system, which we were ready to use in case of trouble. Fortunately, although some minor squabbles broke loose between the sailors and the natives, there was no serious trouble.

My main job was getting the sailors back on board in time to get under way, and that was not easy. One sailor, aided by another, tried to smuggle about ten cartons of cigarettes over, was caught by British customs, and turned over to me. I had to place him under arrest, and he will be court-martialed. Something like that was always happening. Although I only had the watch for 4 hours, I was very exhausted, completely different from the wonderful all day Saturday and Sunday morning. … You see, being Americans, we cannot interfere with the natives, who are on their own pier. Their own police are ineffective, and expect a bribe for keeping order. They are terrified of the British Marines, however, and if they think they are coming, really quiet down.

Well, so ended that little adventure. I think we may go to Haiti next week-end.

Bill ended the letter with a description of the weekend oil explosion and fire that had engulfed the dock in Guantanamo where his ship usually tied up. The flames killed several Cubans working in the area, but other ships moved out safely before the fire intensified.

The *Stoddard's* Caribbean tour continued through the fall of 1951 and into the winter of 1952, with stops in Port au Prince, Haiti, and Culebra, Puerto Rico. It ended in April in Newport, Rhode Island. There, Captain Reich detached from the ship to begin a career in ordnance in Washington, D.C. The next tour would find the *Stoddard* joining the Sixth Fleet for what was billed as a six-month tour of the Mediterranean. Bill hoped it might be shortened to four months so he could return to civilian life and teaching at WPI.

While the ship was in its home port, he spent a welcome leave in Lee. After returning safely to the ship on April 7, he told his mother, "I only wish I were staying out of this for good, since it is unpleasant to come back after being sort of a civilian for a few days!"

The new commanding officer, John Baumeister Jr., had been just a year behind Commander Reich at the U.S. Naval Academy, but he demonstrated a radically different style of leadership, according to Bill. "The new Captain is certainly not the driver Capt. Reich was," he wrote. "He is currently running a contest on the ship for a ship's crest which he wants to get painted on all the boats and things. He is also having a dance band organized and things like that. He really believes in keeping the crew informed."

The two appreciated each other right away. As Bill reported, Baumeister was an MIT graduate with a master's degree in electronics. "If it weren't for the exec who still runs around screaming about all sorts of little things," he added in his note, "we would have an excellent ship."

As he anticipated the sight of land again, Bill said, "It will be good to get ashore and stand on something which will stay still for a little while. We are rolling all the time, but I don't mind the rolling, it is the pitching that really gets me; i.e., when we go up and down like in an elevator."

SAVORING NEW SIGHTS

Late in the day on May 1, 1952, the boy from small-town Lee had his first look at Europe. He shared his thoughts with his mother as if filing a reporter's dispatch on an overseas assignment:

> Well, tonight, just a few minutes ago I got my first glance at Europe. It is just getting dark, and we looked out on the horizon and saw a light and some hills—it is the southwestern point of Portugal. It didn't look much different than any other land I have ever seen from the sea, and it was good to know that the end of our long trip was in sight. At the same time though, there is a sense of lonesomeness realizing that for once this land is not Point Judith, R.I., Cape Hatteras, N.C.,

or even Key Largo, Fla., but a very foreign land some 3,000 miles away. However, it is comforting to know that on that land the people are basically friendly.

They landed in Gibraltar, a British Crown Colony, and Bill found "the rock" underwhelming. "That big rock you see in insurance policies ... is not so tremendous after all. It is 14 miles from Spain to Africa, not just a stone's throw as the maps seem to indicate."

May 1 was also the day Bill was notified of his promotion to full lieutenant. It was a hoped-for honor, but not an automatic one, as he learned of several peers who remained at the lieutenant (j.g.) rank throughout similar deployments.

Life on the *Stoddard* was not all work, and Bill's chronicles of this journey include many sightseeing descriptions as well as a few personal details that bring the reader into the moment with him. While still in Gibraltar, he said:

> I am sitting in the wardroom typing this letter, eating ice cream covered with strawberry jam, and listening to the radio. The European radio has much better programs than at home. There is a British station here, and even the Spanish stations are very nice to listen to, because even though I can't understand them, they have such very fine music. There is a wonderful Spanish concert on now.

His list of ports of call reads like the itinerary for a grand, if slightly offbeat tour of the Mediterranean and Adriatic: Lisbon, Portugal; Cagliari, Sardinia; Cannes, France; Taranto, Syracuse, and Salerno, Italy (with a side trip to Rome); the Free Territory of Trieste (with excursions to the Alps); and Split, Yugoslavia.

But of course, this was no pleasure cruise, a fact made clear when the ship was engaged in military operations with names like BEEHIVE II, in which the Sixth Fleet orchestrated war games played without ammunition. During these maneuvers, Bill would spend nearly sleepless nights on high alert, with the public address system squawking nonstop, as he controlled 16 planes, tracked other ships as they maneuvered into position to protect the beach, screened for submarines, and instructed the planes to raid airfields and intercept incoming raids.

After one scheduled operation, he wrote, "I must certainly say that although the fleet exercises are nightmares, the periods in port sure live up to the Navy's slogan to see the world."

He tried to give his mother a clear sense of what his job entailed, and often sent enclosures with his letters. One note was attached to an annotated magazine image of ships at sea, including an aircraft carrier, a destroyer (with a blue arrow pointing to a boat he labeled DD 566), and several fighter planes. The note said, "In case you wonder what I do and see all day long, this will give you a very good idea. We sail along like this hour after hour ready to pick up any planes that drop off the carrier in landing or taking off. It's very safe indeed for us—but those pilots earn their money."

In September 1952 one plane was lost, setting off a massive search. The plane was thought to be carrying the Secretary of the Navy, who had been watching the Sixth Fleet's maneuvers. Bill's report helped his mother picture the huge operation, which eventually ended with the discovery of the plane's wreckage by the Italian Navy.

> An Operational Immediate Priority message came in saying that a big plane had been lost near Sardinia. At first we thought it was the plane that the Secretary of the Navy was on, since he has been here with the fleet for several days watching the maneuvers. However, I guess it wasn't, but things sure started to happen. They have set up a gigantic search for the plane. At present we are a unit of a scouting line proceeding across the ocean in a line 50 miles long! So you can guess from that the size of the force; and we are only a fraction of the total ships here! If you can imagine a line of ships extending from Lee to Springfield all heading in the same direction in perfect line of bearing, then you can picture the size of our maneuvers. We have all sorts of special lookouts stationed and there is much looking around. I am under the impression that there must be someone pretty important on the plane to have all this stir, for I don't think the plane was actually too big, and was a military job. They have called out everything, even tankers from Sardinia to look for it, and the Air Force's planes from Africa and Germany have been alerted. I have

seen them lose planes before, when they sent out about 4 destroyers and several squadrons of search planes, but never anything like this.

It is my job as Operations Officer, to keep track of all the messages about affairs like this, and be up to the minute on the overall picture, which makes life quite interesting at times, although it is also a huge headache during big maneuvers, since things change extremely fast. You may have seen the people in the movies with big maps and lots of lines and pins on them keeping track of maneuvers—that is what I do most of the time.

His letters helped his family see Europe through his fresh eyes. Early in his tour, Bill experienced the full spectrum of poverty and wealth in post-war Europe. After the British order of Gibraltar and the cleanliness of Lisbon, the poor living conditions and extent of war damage in Sardinia was eye-opening for the sailor who had remained stateside during World War II:

Yesterday was the first time I had ever seen the destruction of war. … This is certainly an education, if nothing else, especially in what these people are up against with the Communists. The people who stand up to them are really brave. It is impossible to realize the terror of a street riot or the passion of a Communist rally until you see a place like this. And after seeing the burned-out buildings, bomb holes and caves, there is certainly a great deal to be done in our prayers for peace.

Other letters offered observations and opinions on what he found ashore. "Today was National French communion Sunday, and there were huge parades and demonstrations everywhere," he wrote from Cannes. "I guess in France either they are extremely good Christians, or else they are Communists."

"We had a grand tour through Monaco and the lower Alps," he recounted at the end of May. "This is certainly a very beautiful country." Sharing his wonder with his mother, he added, "Monaco is a page out of an operetta—it's a storybook kingdom if ever one existed—located in incredibly mountainous country—with police & guards dressed in fantastically elaborate costumes. It is really a dream world. I would never have believed such a thing existed in the world if I hadn't seen it!"

On board ship, Bill's estimation of the commanding officer continued to rise, though the ship's executive officer (never named) was another story. In June he wrote:

> The Captain is as quiet as ever, and isn't bad to get along with at all. He has a good sense of humor, and is easy to get along with. The executive officer gets more stupid every day, and is becoming very melancholy. He is impossible sometimes. Some days I feel sorry for him, and other times could bite his head off. He does absolutely nothing, and always is complaining about something or other.

Everyone on board had multiple roles. A member of the ship's court for court-martial proceedings and the person responsible for administering the advancement-in-rate examinations, Bill was also in charge of what he simply called "Education," producing for the crew one-page summaries of the next port's history and significant features.

Syracuse in Sicily, he noted in one of his education pieces, is one of the great cities of antiquity. He pointed out the ruins of amphitheaters where lions ate Christians and how Archimedes helped the city endure a two-year Roman siege. Syracuse, he concluded, "was probably well known as about the biggest and best liberty port in the Med, but we are about two or three thousand years too late."

He was almost single-minded in his desire to get to Rome. "I think I shall have an excellent chance now to get up to Rome when we get to Italy," he told his mother. "The chaplain says he will try to fix us up with an audience with the Pope, and that should be wonderful." From Salerno, Rome was a four-day excursion, and Bill passed up other side trips, even one to Paris, to maintain his priority for this one.

Father McGroarty, the ship's chaplain, more than delivered on his promise. Bill Grogan had two audiences with Pope Pius XII, as he shared with his mother:

> I shall have much to write about Rome and more to tell you about when I see you—it is certainly an incredible place. There were many

American tourists there. The history behind it, and the closeness of the church is unbelievable. It certainly is worth any number of years of history classes just to visit the place. I saw the Pope again, for a second time, and had a picture taken with him, which I shall send when I can find something to fit it in.

His delight in his trips while on liberty helped to ease the intensity of the ship's scheduled operations. During one operation, the usual stresses were exacerbated by the climate. While sailing off the shores of Tripoli, Bill described the situation with a reporter's eye for detail:

> To add to the troubles of the operations we have had the hottest spell since we have been over here. Operating all week off Africa, near Tripoli the temperature has really been something. The water temperature is almost 90°, and the air was extremely humid. It never cooled off at night, and everything was literally dripping wet all night—the decks and people alike. It was about the worst week we have ever spent. All through June and July the weather was cool and beautiful, and I guess we were much cooler and better off than the people at home as far as the weather went. However, when we went down to Sicily it grew very warm, and last week was really the climax.

While he could complain about the heat near Africa or Sicily, Bill was thankful not to be in a region like Korea, where the operations were not orchestrated war games—they used real ammunition. "So all in all I am quite lucky to be sitting around here in quiet Italian and French ports," he wrote, "no matter how bad it is to be away from home, it is not like being in Korea."

Following operations off Tripoli, Bill was happy to report in late August that "this morning we entered the much cooler Adriatic Sea, and now are in Brindisi, where there is a beautiful breeze blowing and it is extremely pleasant once more. I hope it keeps up this way."

The town of Brindisi was the site of perhaps the most-told story of Bill Grogan's military years. For reasons unknown, his letters home omit this particular tale. According to several sources, when Bill and his fellow officers were granted liberty in this southern Italian city, they supported the local bars' business quite heartily. After a night out, they organized mock chariot races with some local horses—or mules, the details differ somewhat—while the local townspeople watched and cheered. Although Bill knew Latin but spoke little, if any, Italian, near the end of the evening, he enthusiastically invited the townspeople to visit him on the ship the next day.

The next morning, they took him up on his offer and arrived at the gangplank. Hundreds of them. Bill, still asleep, was awakened by urgent knocking on his door. The captain had left the ship to visit a lady friend outside town and the executive officer had locked himself in his room in a bout of depression. Lt. Grogan was next in command. How should he respond?

As he pulled on his dress whites and shook the fog out of his brain, he told the messenger to set up tables with cake, invite the locals on board, and offer ice cream to the children.

As American military property, the USS *Stoddard* was off limits to foreign nationals. Still, the townspeople came aboard, the sailors gave them tours, and the children loved the ice cream. But when the captain returned, Bill knew he was likely to be court-martialed.

As they awaited the captain's return, word reached the *Stoddard* that the Commander of the entire Sixth Fleet, Vice Admiral John Cassady, wanted to see its acting commander. A boat was dispatched and Bill and another officer were taken to see him, ready to receive their punishment. Instead, Cassady presented them with a decoration in recognition of the good will they'd generated through the impromptu open house. As the story goes, the Admiral said, "This is *exactly* what we wanted to do. We want to make friends with these people, and by God, you got it right."

In fact, during his overseas tour Bill observed generally positive responses to Americans from people throughout southern Europe:

> Once convinced that you are [not British but] American, the change in attitude is amazing. People will stop what they are doing, and walk with you down the street to point out a place, or want to know if you know their cousin in New York, etc. etc. and in general do all they can to help you out. A sailor of French descent in France, or of

Italian descent in Italy is really a king, especially if they speak the language. The people treat them as if they were natives of the town just returned home. It is the unreachable ambition of most of these people to sometime see the USA, but most of them know they never will, and have to continue watching it in the movies.

Bill encountered a chillier response to Americans when the *Stoddard* reached Communist-controlled Split, Yugoslavia, in September 1952, near the end of his time at sea. The ship was joined there by the rest of the Sixth Fleet, including an aircraft carrier and a squadron of planes. As he reported, "Yesterday afternoon we gave Tito a huge air demonstration out off the coast here. It was really something—fire bombs, rockets, etc. They put up over 60 planes in practically no time at all." The Yugoslavian military replied in-kind, with an earthbound show of force: a vast parade of its ground troops.

In the city of Split, Bill reported speaking with several ordinary citizens, not all of whom were enthusiastic about Communism. In a whisper, one man said to him that he didn't want a Communist government because he believed in God. The city was "cleaner than Italy" and had mostly repaired its wartime damage. The trip was a reported success and it served as the final major event for Bill's time overseas.

By the time the *Stoddard* returned to Newport in mid-October, Bill had decided he would request early release from active duty. Still a day or two from port, he wrote to the Secretary of the Navy, following protocol by sending his letter through his commanding officer and the chief of naval personnel.

He made the case that he had completed more than 20 of his maximum obligated 24 months of service, and he wanted to be home before Christmas. "The winter-spring college term starts in January," he wrote, "and it would be highly desirable to spend some time prior to the beginning of the term in preparation for the work. It is therefore respectfully requested that if possible I be released from active duty by mid-December (after twenty-two (22) months duty), thereby enabling me to prepare for and resume my academic schedule."

This time his request was granted, and he made it home in time to send out a few Christmas cards. The academic calendar didn't have classes beginning until late January, so he probably had the chance to enjoy the type of homecoming he had envisioned when he wrote, "I want to get home for a while and just sit around, hanging on the sofa for a few weeks and sleeping!"

Back on Campus

Bill Grogan's return to campus for the spring semester of 1953 did not end his relationship with the Naval Reserve. He remained on inactive status through the 1960s, but continued to serve in other capacities.

George Saltus '51 had known Bill since 1946, when George was a freshman and Bill a new graduate student back from his wartime service. Bill had suggested he consider the Navy Reserve for his military service. Saltus went on to serve in Korea, after which, in 1951, he received his EE degree from WPI. He was asked, would he stay on for a master's degree, given the offer of a graduate assistant position? "You betcha!" was his response.

The professor he assisted was Bill Grogan, who had asked Saltus to run a few of his afternoon labs while he was deployed on the *Stoddard*. The two Navy men hit it off well, Saltus recalled.

As a reservist, Bill approached Saltus at one point to help him teach math to Navy personnel. That went so well, he said, that when the Worcester electrical contractors union approached WPI for a basic electronics course, the two Navy men were happy to provide a one-hour weekly night class for a year or two. Some 30 to 40 students attended, and the two instructors gave them an entry test to assess their knowledge. They found the electricians knew about electrical power but not electronics. At the end of the course, they gave the students the same test to confirm they had mastered the materials.

Their findings? "Yes, they had learned something," said Saltus. "They were all happy." As were Saltus and Grogan. "We made good money on that," Saltus said.

NAVY CONSULTANT

Bill spent several summers working for General Electric in Pittsfield, not far from his family in Lee. That first summer of 1953, he served as a consulting engineer on a defense research project investigating thyratron applications in sonic trigger circuits. Thyratrons are gas-filled discharge chambers with cathode filaments, typically used as high-power electrical switches that can handle greater currents than hard-vacuum tubes. GE published his confidential research results, "Analog Simulation of the MK 35 Torpedo," in September 1953 as part of its internal technical information series.

In 1954 he began working on the Atlas weapons system as a project engineer and eventually served as sub-chairman of the Atlas missile study group's guidance phase, which that fall published "New Precision in Analog-Digital Conversion." Over the next six years, he produced a series of ten classified articles in the General Electric Technical Information Series, dealing primarily with missile guidance and control. He consulted for the MK44 Torpedo Transistorization Program and also the Tartar Missile Guidance System development.

With Bill's successful work on naval ordnance systems at GE, it came as no surprise in 1962 when the Navy asked him to serve as a personal consultant to the chief of the Special Naval Task Force on Surface Missile Systems. The request came from none other than Eli Reich, the demanding captain from Bill's days on the USS *Stoddard.* Now an admiral in the Bureau of Naval Weapons. Reich had kept in touch with Bill in the intervening decade.

Working officially as a consultant for Howard Research Corporation, Bill evaluated proposals for the Navy to acquire new weapons systems. Among the systems then in development was the Typhon missile, which incorporated a new phased array radar system, AN/SPG-59, for wide-area air defense against Soviet missiles.

In 1964 the Applied Physics Laboratory (APL) of Johns Hopkins University asked Bill to become a member of a special Navy commission tasked with conducting a high-level examination of "the long-range educational needs of scientifically and technically oriented personnel with the Navy, especially those assigned to the Navy's mission operations," as he explained to his department chair in a memo that December. The work would take him out of Worcester about two days a month, on average.

The new consulting assignment dovetailed nicely with his previous work at Bell Labs, which he'd completed only a few months earlier. "Educational problems involved in multi-nation technical operations may also be considered," Bill wrote about his new assignment, "but the initial phases will concern the graduate education of specialized officer personnel."

The commission's work began almost immediately in Bermuda, and then moved aboard the USS *Norton Sound*, an experimental guided missile ship. Bill was particularly interested to visit the ship as it housed the pre-production prototype of the AN/SPG-59 system he had studied for Admiral Reich. Though the Navy had canceled the Typhon system in 1963, it allowed an engineering test of the radar system aboard the *Norton Sound* to continue.

He continued his work with APL the following year, but added a new responsibility. Together with his former student Jim Demetry '58, who was then attending the U.S. Naval Postgraduate School in California as a civilian faculty fellow, Bill joined the AN/SPG-59 Radar Advisory Group. Convened as "an ad hoc technical group to assess the overall current status and potential of the USS *Norton Sound* engineering test program," the group was asked to advise the director of the Surface Missile System Project on "the future conduct of this program." Its high-powered membership included representatives from Bell Labs, Westinghouse, Sperry Gyroscope, Hughes Aircraft, Raytheon, RCA, and GE. Selected to chair the group was Bill Grogan.

In the space of one week in early November 1965, the group met at the Johns Hopkins APL facility in Maryland for three days of orientation and then caught an overnight flight to California for briefings at Port Hueneme, where the *Norton Sound* was anchored. On the fifth day, the group deliberated in a closed session to determine its response.

"It is desired that the group in its report should include matters of fact, matters of opinion, and such recommendations as are deemed appropriate," noted the group's missions and task document.

Seen as impartial third parties, Bill and his group were asked to make a final recommendation on whether the government should continue to fund the phased-array radar system. They submitted their confidential report, co-authored by William R. Grogan, in December. Looking back, Jim Demetry succinctly summarized it: "… built and tested by Johns Hopkins and Westinghouse, it couldn't be made to work reliably." After reviewing the program's history and failures, and remaining mindful of the years of funding that had already been invested in the project, the group recommended that the Navy end the radar system project and not "throw good money after bad."

Ben Sarver, who had replaced Admiral Reich as director of the Surface Missiles System Project, sent Bill a congratulatory note to express his gratitude and appreciation "for the very effective and workmanlike way in which you undertook the tasks of chairman," and described the final report as "a very professional and extremely valuable piece of work."

Washington continued to call on Bill's knowledge of engineering education. Before he had completed the radar system report, he attended his first meeting of President Lyndon Johnson's Commission on the Reduction of the Draft. In his role as a civilian, he joined representatives from the Army, Navy, Marine Corps, Air Force, Department of Defense, and Department of Health, Education, and Welfare to study possible educational incentives to make voluntary military service more attractive.

Traveling to the Pentagon about once a week, Bill hoped the study— one of several contributing to Department of Defense discussions about reducing the military draft at the time—would focus on the development of programs to fill the need for officers and technical personnel with highly specialized engineering and technical backgrounds.

Eventually renamed the President's Military Manpower Policy Board, the group found its work quickly eclipsed by the escalation of the Vietnam War in 1966.

Ever ready to continue learning about the military applications of the electronics he had studied so closely, Bill attended annual seminars at the Naval War College in Newport for years. But as his responsibilities at WPI increased, he could not maintain the required level of participation in the Reserves. Within the Navy, said longtime friend Bob Fitzgerald, Bill was "a teacher, an engineer, a patriot." But "one of Bill's great regrets," Fitzgerald continued, "was that he did not stay in the Navy to reach retirement status." He officially transferred into "retired reserve" on December 1, 1968.

Bill learned from the military much about team building and the nature of men. Colleague and friend Lance Schachterle recalled one piece of military wisdom Bill shared with him. He said that in the Navy, if an officer who was doing a really good job on a ship applied for a more senior position, the captain might choose to keep the officer in his current post because of the value he brought to that job. But typically, that officer, wanting to move up the ranks, would then apply for a more senior position on a rival ship and, more than likely, he would receive it.

"So you were foolish not to promote the person," recalled Schachterle, "because otherwise you would not only lose him, but his skills would then be contributing to another ship's efficiency. That seemed to me to be a shrewd point."

In November 1945, the Navy's Midshipman School published its first peacetime yearbook. It included a reflective epilogue. "In the process of becoming Naval Officers, men have been taught many things which will be of great help, not only in the Naval service, but in civilian capacities," it said. "The Ensign who returns to civilian life will be a better citizen and a better patriot because of courses such as Naval Law and Naval Leadership. This training has not been in vain, nor has it been a wasted portion in the lives of hundreds of thousands of young Navy Reservists."

His military experience proved to be a lifelong gift for Bill Grogan. At sea or on land, he learned to manage men, pursue goals by working within (and sometimes around) prescribed authority structures, and, when he deemed it necessary, maintain a healthy respect for hierarchy.

CHAPTER SIX

Restructuring the Brotherhood

Give, expecting nothing thereof.
—Phi Kappa Theta motto

WHEN VISITORS ENTER the Phi Kappa Theta house on Institute Road in Worcester, they can't miss a large plaque honoring Bill Grogan in the hallway, many historical documents, photos, and trophies, and the words Passion, Dedication, Integrity, Humility, and Leadership mounted on the TV room wall. What they will miss is the scent of stale beer. By student choice, the fraternity is a dry house. Climb the back stairs, and you can read the fraternity's pledge, as the words are stenciled on the risers:

> The mission of Phi Kappa Theta is to foster a brotherhood of exceptional men and guide them to become individuals who routinely display passion and dedication in their endeavors, always maintain integrity and humility, and show the ability to lead through influence.

The William R. Grogan Chapter House looks nothing like the *Animal House* stereotype, but it hasn't always been so clean and well-ordered.

Above: *The Phi Kappa Theta William R. Grogan Chapter House at 26 Institute Road.*

Everywhere you look, the house reflects the changes and reincarnations that Phi Kappa Theta underwent during Bill Grogan's relationship with the fraternity, which lasted more than 72 years.

Bill's involvement with Theta Kappa Phi started not long after he arrived on campus in the fall of 1942. He pledged just before Christmas, during the last traditional fraternity rush season before WPI became a Navy V-12 program site. At that time, Theta Kappa Phi was the only fraternity at WPI that would accept Catholic students. It had been chartered in November 1935 with the help of Dr. Charles Burns, a local dentist, and other prominent Worcester businessmen, many of them alumni of the College of the Holy Cross. Just over 20 percent of WPI students identified themselves as Catholic in those years, and in Bill's freshman class, that figure rose to 28 percent.

Encouraged by a recent encyclical from Pope Pius XII promoting lay service to Catholic youth of the world, Burns and his colleagues had met with a group of WPI students organized as the Friars Club. They were seeking "mature guidance" for their "problems of finance and direction," according to a 1954 report. Creating the 11th chapter of the national fraternity Theta Kappa Phi gave the students not just an official association with a national organization, but membership in an international movement of Catholic students, Pax Romana.

Two years later, this group of supportive adults formed the Aquinas Association to help the young chapter manage "insoluble housing difficulties," as an annual report noted. The new organization purchased the building at 26 Institute Road that remains the Lambda Chapter's William R. Grogan Chapter House today.

AN ARISTOCRACY OF THE SOUL

The chapter's motto remains "give, expecting nothing thereof." But recognizing that a desire to be the best men on campus would give the fraternity a good reputation, though perhaps appear too exclusive, one of its "most distinguished and learned" alumni, John Wright, Bishop of Worcester (1950–59), reassured new members that this ambitious desire was not antidemocratic. In his message, printed in an early pledge manual, Wright said, "the foundations of a decent democracy must be continually nourished by an aristocracy of the soul, an aristocracy of the mind, an aristocracy of moral values. ... You cannot rest content with equality with the crowd."

Based on the chapter's trophy collection, which today crowds a mantelpiece and bookshelves in the dining room, members of Theta Kappa Phi were not overly concerned about earning too many accolades for their chapter. During Bill's senior year and the year after, "Theta Kap" won the National Efficiency Award for Chapter Improvement and Cooperation. Members or alumni regularly received the National Distinguished Service Award.

Theta Kap was one of only four fraternities at WPI that remained open during the years of World War II. With most students participating in the V-12 program and thus required to live in Navy-regulated campus dormitories, the Aquinas Association turned to the area's civilian population for sustenance, renting out rooms to non-members to make ends meet.

After the war ended in 1945, students came in greater numbers. As Bill recounted, those who were veterans were "ideal fraternity brothers," and much more responsible than other undergraduates. One year, he said, the chapter president was a high-ranking officer who had flown B-29s. Another member, recalled Bob Fitzgerald '53, fought in the Battle of the Bulge.

SEIZING THE MOMENT

His military service completed, Bill returned to WPI to begin graduate study in electrical engineering while working as an instructor. He also resumed Theta Kap activities with his hallmark enthusiasm, which he now brought to the role of faculty advisor.

One of his responsibilities was to vet new employees, as John Burgarella '50 well remembers. A sophomore living at the fraternity, he applied for a dishwashing job. "He interviewed me very carefully," Burgarella said.

For Bill, there were two key questions: "Are you conscientious?" and "Do you need the job?" To make it clear that this job was necessary, and not just for extra money, Burgarella said, he agreed to answer Bill's pointed question, "How much money do you have in the bank?"

"I got the job," he reported, and was soon labeled a "fussy guy," because "I insisted on washing the outside of the cooking pots as well as the inside."

As the fraternity's faculty advisor, Bill was mature, enthusiastic, and "gung ho about the fraternity," he continued. "There was a lot of singing around the piano. One song ended with the words 'and the old man died,' just as the mantel clock chimed. It was so classic." Bill then recorded the song on a wire recorder, which used a spool of wire instead of tape, and the fraternity brothers could play it back on the same device.

Despite his busy schedule in the final weeks of classes in early June 1947, Bill hatched an idea after reading an article in the newspaper about Assumption College's graduation speaker. As he noted in a letter to his parents, "I saw on the front page that Cardinal Gerlier, Primate Cardinal of France and Archbishop of Lyon, would be here this week. A ponderous idea struck me: wouldn't he make a wonderful honorary member!"

With only a week's notice, Bill—along with the fraternity's national executive, George Uihlein '45, and several other fraternity members— jumped through a number of administrative hoops, working their way up the Assumption College hierarchy and over to the cardinal's secretary, who had received their invitation to the cardinal in French, thanks to translation work from a Theta Kap member from Assumption.

Two other brothers wrote a press release, and one sent it to his father, a *Boston Herald* correspondent, in hopes of getting the story on the Associated Press wire. "This is quite a deal if we can swing it," Bill told his parents.

It was, indeed, quite a deal. The cardinal accepted their invitation. The brothers were all invited to a reception for him in his suite at the Sheraton, and then they attended a banquet for 400 of the area's Franco-Americans. The *Worcester Daily Telegram* ran a story about the newest member of Theta Kappa Phi, with a photo of the prelate surrounded by his WPI brothers.

The day after the banquet, Bill began a 3,000-mile round-trip journey to the Theta Kappa Phi national convention in Rolla, Missouri, flying from Boston to Washington, D.C., and driving the rest of the way. He concluded his letter home with the understatement, "A big day tomorrow, and every day for the next week," adding the postscript, "Happy Birthday, Mom!"

Less than two months later, Bill would celebrate his own birthday, and the fraternity's faculty advisor would turn 23.

THE GOLDEN YEARS

In the late 1940s and early '50s, WPI students tended to be older than typical undergraduates; in some cases, they were older than their professors. So when Bill Grogan spent time in the chapter house, visitors didn't always recognize him as the faculty advisor.

But he and Uihlein, both unmarried and only a year apart at WPI, would have dinner there and tutor students struggling with their classes. Though Bill's apartment on the top floor of WPI's Alden Memorial was just a few blocks away, "George and Bill seemed to be there all the time," said Fitzgerald. "Therefore, they each became 'just one of the boys.'"

"But Bill was a little different," he continued. "Yes, he was one of the boys, happy to go out to the Boynton for a beer, but he was almost always able to give you personal mentoring. Anybody who was having some problems, he would tend to not only help there, but generally give guidance."

Bill's commitment to his fraternity brothers yielded great dividends. The Aquinas Association annual report from 1954 highlights the successful student members that year: "The achievements of the fraternity have fully justified the confidence placed in the enterprise by the Aquinas Association members," it concluded. Theta Kap brothers were members of every undergraduate honor society, 28 out of 36 newspaper staffers, the yearbook editor, presidents of both the junior and senior classes, chairman of the Tech Council of Presidents, and captains of the varsity teams in football, basketball, and baseball, not to mention seven of the 11 starting players of the undefeated 1954 football team.

"Ahh, the '50s!" wrote Bill to a fraternity brother from the Class of 1960. "I often refer to that period as the 'Golden Years'—life in college was good, friendships solid, and the Kap was great." With a total membership of more than 80 (not all residential, but most on a meal plan), Theta Kappa Phi was the largest fraternity on campus in the mid-1950s.

Whether Catholic, Protestant, or Jewish, nearly all WPI students were members of a fraternity in those years, and many depended on them for housing, as dormitory rooms were mostly limited to freshmen. Saturday morning classes encouraged students to stay on campus on weekends, so the fraternities also provided the school's social life.

"We were active in the community," said Len Dutram '59. "We would host parties for orphans at Christmas time, do fundraising for various causes like the hospital, a lot like now."

While the fellowship was fine, the chapter house needed constant attention. The alumni board wrestled with the expenses of keeping the house standing, noting a termite invasion in 1948, the need for a complete rewiring job for fire safety, a multitude of updated kitchen appliances, and the very welcome addition of a second shower for the 28 residents. As a member of the Aquinas Association's finance committee, Grogan was certainly well aware of the financial pressures inherent in a growing enterprise. Beyond utilities, laundry, and payments for the bathroom renovation, regular expenses included wages for a maid and "linen boys."

Bill invented numerous ways for fraternity brothers to get out of the house. Dutram joined Theta Kap in the fall of 1955 and remembered a variety of outings, all organized by Bill. He would drive with a group to go skiing at Cannon Mountain in New Hampshire. When the day was done, Dutram recalled, Bill would open the trunk of his car (always a Ford) and administer, with a grin, what he called "slope medicine"— some kind of cherry liqueur—to ward off the chill. Once the parking lot had emptied out and all the other skiers had left, Bill would say it was time for "take-off practice," which involved revving up the car, sliding across the icy surface, and skidding sideways into "humongous" piles of snow that surrounded the lot.

"It would make a real 'phumph' sound," Dutram said with a laugh. That activity was "about as risqué as I'd ever seen Bill."

Other excursions organized by Bill included trips to New York City. He and George Uihlein would take Dutram and another brother downtown to visit Joe King's German-American Rathskeller on Third Avenue and 17th Street. Its walls decorated with theatrical programs and celebrity photographs, the restaurant was perfect for the group from Theta Kappa Phi. Known as the "fraternity house of the nation," with a menu featuring such German specialties as sauerbraten, wiener schnitzel, and bratwurst, the restaurant was also famous for its large steins of German beer. Drunk slowly, the beer would go flat, so guests would race to finish their "seidel," which held about a quart.

After a seidel or two, most patrons would launch into singing German songs together. One that the group enjoyed, said Dutram, was the Schnitzelbank song, designed to teach German-American children basic words by repeating them again and again—from cobbler's bench and wagon wheel to fat sow, tall man, and pile of manure—using pictures on wall posters to help people remember the words. And, of course, the night wasn't complete without a rendition of the famous student drinking song, "Gaudeamus Igitur."

"Bill was a wonderful guy to be with," said Dutram fondly, "a very easy guy to be around."

ANOTHER HONORARY MEMBER

Worcester in the 1950s had its share of celebrity visitors. On October 2, 1958, the increasingly popular Catholic politician Massachusetts Senator John F. Kennedy arrived at Assumption College with his wife, Jacqueline, and brother Robert to dedicate a new science center in memory of their older brother, Lt. Joseph P. Kennedy. Later, at the

Worcester Armory in Lincoln Square, Sen. Kennedy was the honored guest at a pinning ceremony, where he became an honorary member of WPI's Catholic fraternity, Theta Kappa Phi. Before the ceremony, in which chapter president Don Ferrari '59 presented the pin to the senator, his classmate Len Dutram had the opportunity to sit and chat with the Kennedys.

A still photo of this historic event has long decorated the walls of the fraternity, but more than a half century later, a brief home movie of the occasion surfaced when a brother who had attended the event cleaned out his attic.

A TRUE MERGER

Senator Kennedy entered into the Theta Kappa Phi brotherhood in the last months of the fraternity's existence. His pinning ceremony was held just a few weeks after two separate national conventions voted to merge Theta Kappa Phi with Phi Kappa. Both fraternities held similar ideals, recruited Catholic men, and on a few campuses, competed quite fiercely for them. By the end of April 1959, they would be one organization.

"I had only heard of Phi Kappa on some of our large campuses where we both had chapters," Bill recalled in an interview on the fraternity's history published in its member magazine, *The Temple.* As vice president of Theta Kappa Phi's national board of trustees at the time, he knew that the two fraternities had started conversations back in 1933, but had suspended serious discussions until 1955. That was the year Theta Kappa Phi authorized the national council to take another look at consolidation.

"We began to talk about what it would take to actually do this," Bill told *The Temple.* "There were many heated conversations on the officer level about how exactly to do this, to merge." Phi Kappa, the older of the two fraternities (founded in 1889 at Brown University), also had a much older leadership team and numerous alumni groups—and crucially, far more financial resources. Theta Kappa Phi (founded at Lehigh University in 1919) had a much younger board that was "more dynamic," according to Greg Stein (City College of New York '70), the fraternity's unofficial historian who headed up the Phi Kappa Theta Foundation. With leaner staffing, they were more "hands on," he said, visiting chapters rather than managing from afar.

"The senior leadership of each organization wanted it because they saw the importance of blending the experienced leadership with the young enthusiasm," said Bill. In April 1957, national officers from both fraternities held a conference to discuss whether a merger was possible. They drew up more formal plans the following February, and asked chapters across the country to vote for or against a merger.

Delegates from both fraternities held simultaneous conventions in early September 1958 at The Ohio State University in Columbus. It was a close vote.

Bill, himself, felt "kind of cool on the idea," he reported. "There were only several votes that kept this thing passing. It was no overwhelming landslide." But the merger was approved, and on September 8 a news release announced the decision to form "one national fraternity for Catholic men to be called Phi Kappa Theta." The news was distributed to several national fraternity organizations, deans of men at colleges with chapters, chapter officers, chaplains, and alumni, where lists existed.

Phi Kappa's 59 chapters had 1,200 active members and more than 10,000 alumni. Theta Kappa Phi had 26 chapters with 750 active members and over 7,000 alumni. Both fraternities' executive directors would continue in those positions, and the new board, jointly headed by Frank Flick of Theta Kap and Pierre Lavedan of Phi Kappa, would have eight representatives from each fraternity. They would work to complete the consolidation by May 1959.

Ever the communicator, Bill knew it was important to control the message and quickly share as much information as was available. He kept a draft copy of a release, which included this note to George Uihlein (most likely from himself): "Think it good to get even this brief note to our chapter supervisors, etc., and follow with other material so they will get news first from us."

Once the new national fraternity was voted into existence, all the other details needed to be worked out. How could they combine the two sets of rituals, badges, coats of arms, and colors, all of which held special meaning to existing members and alumni?

A very careful blending ensued, and the decision on the colors involves a Bill Grogan story. As Phi Kappa Theta's executive director from the 1970s Robert Wilcox recalled, Bill was assigned the task of finding colors acceptable to both groups. Phi Kappa's colors were gold and purple, while Theta Kap's were white, silver, and red. The board had chosen white and gold, but debated an overwhelming number of shades of red, as Bill later told Nick Scalera, a fellow board member in the late 1960s.

"Bill frequented a restaurant in downtown Worcester," Wilcox said, located across the street from a store that sold Catholic goods. In the window was a color photograph of Boston's Richard Cardinal Cushing wearing a double-tiered full-length cape, all in muted red. Not the bright red typical of more contemporary cardinal robes, this style was traditionally worn during papal election conclaves.

He ran into the store and asked, "What color is the Cardinal's robe?" And the answer was "cardinal purple." He had found the perfect compromise. While it looked red, the color's name was purple.

Grogan wasted no time, Wilcox related. "He borrowed the photo, took it to the stationery store next door, and had them pull out their color wheel to match it. Then he bought several sheets of paper in that color, cut them into squares and stapled them to letters sent to all 70 chapters that said 'this is the official cardinal purple color; please find ink to match.'"

"It was the phraseology," said Scalera. "Bill's genius was to find a solution, even if in words only."

The charter day to commemorate the consolidation nationwide was set for April 29, 1959, the date that Phi Kappa began in 1889. Events were held around the country, starting the weekend before the official date. Bill traveled to RPI's campus in Troy, N.Y., where both fraternities had chapters, to present to their leaders the charter of the new organization at a special dinner.

At WPI's Massachusetts Lambda Chapter, Len Dutram, then a senior, was not in favor of the merger. "I was sternly against it; I thought we would lose our alumni base," he said. But Bill, in his wise way of recognizing students with leadership capabilities, asked him to organize the charter day celebration anyway.

There would be a celebratory tea held at the fraternity house. With little expertise in organizing tea parties, Dutram knew he would need to call in some heavy artillery. Where else to turn but to the military presence on campus? The wife of the professor of military science, Col. Charles Burner, had planned such events many times before and took command of the situation. Mrs. Burner brought in the silver service used for faculty wives' teas, contacted the bakery, and ensured all the details were accounted for. They had tea, champagne, and petit fours. "We did things right," said Len with some pride.

Beyond the formal tea party, however, the brothers held their own ceremony—a wake for Theta Kappa Phi. Someone ordered special cocktail napkins from Denholm's, a local department store. Imprinted in black letters was "Requiesce in Pace," Latin for "rest in peace."

Of all U.S. fraternity consolidations, the combination of Phi Kappa and Theta Kappa Phi came to be known as the only "true" fraternity merger, because the new blended traditions and coats of arms demonstrated that neither organization had absorbed the other. In addition, the new name retained all the letters of both fraternities.

MAKING IT WORK

In addition to helping engineer the merger, Bill served two consecutive terms as president of the new organization, from 1961 to 1965. During those years, the initial 50/50 split of board members representing each fraternity began to change. "It was a balancing act," said Phi Kappa Theta's Greg Stein. "He made the merger work." Added Scalera, who first met Bill as a fellow board member in 1969, "Bill would hold us spellbound with stories about the inner workings of their discussions—the areas of sensitivities on both sides. It took a dynamic leader like Bill to bring things together."

One approach he took during his presidency was to introduce the Quo Vadis movement into the fraternity by establishing retreats where the members would come together once a year for self-reflection and introspection. The Latin "quo vadis" means "where are you going?" and that would be the underlying question in the annual gatherings. As Scalera recalled, the national board would have a Quo Vadis gathering to ask, "Are we remaining true to the values on which this fraternity was formed?"

"It promoted the ideals of brotherhood," he said. "He was engaging in servant leadership," a concept he strongly supported. Asking about the fraternity's values "was a creative way to get at those old traditions that die hard." Quo Vadis Weekends are now established programs for chapters across the country.

A Fraternity of Catholic Heritage

Within a few years of the merger, Bill found himself presiding over its convention and pressing for yet more change. That year, on the campus of the University of Georgia, a new chapter had wanted to recruit a Protestant man. Then a student at the university, Wilcox and his officers wrote to the national office requesting an exception.

In the months leading up to the 1967 convention, Grogan argued that a fraternity formed in the years of prejudice against Catholics could not, in good conscience, perpetuate this exclusionary policy. It was time to drop the Catholics-only clause from the constitution. He asked Jack Bresnahan '68 to come to Washington to present this proposal from the floor. Although a reluctant public speaker, Jack agreed, because "Bill said I had to." There must have been 300 brothers there.

When the time came to consider the proposal, Wilcox said, the Franciscan chaplain from Georgia stood up and spoke about the Protestant student who wanted to join the fraternity. He said the student was a good man who exemplified the fraternity's principles; his admission would benefit the organization by opening its doors to non-Catholics. As a priest, his words carried considerable weight.

The proposal passed. Phi Kappa Theta was no longer the national Catholic fraternity, but a fraternity of Catholic heritage.

"Bill was definitely supportive of the change," said Wilcox. In his advocacy for it, added Scalera, he focused "on the meaning and spirit of brotherhood."

After completing his final term as president, Bill remained on the board for another six years. He stepped away from the national organization in 1971, but gladly supported its executive directors in Worcester when asked. Having overseen the birth and early development of the new fraternal organization, he needed all his time and energy to focus on the emergence of a new WPI curriculum.

SELECTIVITY, SECRECY, AND SERVICE

The first time Greg Stein heard Bill Grogan speak, it was at the fraternity's national management school, held on the University of Detroit campus. It was August 1968; the topic was psychological hazing. Bill was very much against it.

"It was a very powerful speech with immediate impact," recalled Stein, who also remembered many topics of Bill's speeches in subsequent decades. "Most of Bill's speeches had impact," he said. "His presence in the room was overwhelming. There was almost an aura surrounding him. He was a very powerful speaker."

The year after Bill's memorable presentation, he addressed the same theme in a "Faculty Pen" column published in *Tech News* as the new school year (and rushing season) got under way. While he would remain on the national board of Phi Kappa Theta for another two years, he took a longer-term view for fraternities of the future.

"I have always been in favor of the fraternity concept of campus living for those students who wished to participate in it," his column began. Drawing on the keynote speech he'd given the previous month at Phi Kappa Theta's 80th anniversary conference, but broadening his remarks to all fraternities at WPI, Bill wrote that the fraternity system at WPI and at colleges across the country needed to become more "responsive to changing attitudes and a changing campus environment."

This article and speeches he gave at a number of occasions outlined his thoughts on how best to organize—and in the future, reorganize—fraternities to keep them relevant for undergraduates whose futures would embrace the late 20th and early 21st centuries. These ideas became the foundation for his later efforts to reform his own fraternity.

"There are great potential benefits in the fraternity concept," he continued in his *Tech News* column, "but it is with a growing sense of disappointment that one observes the gap between the fraternity concept and the reality of operational situations."

To bridge this gap, Bill put forward "three topics which I feel need immediate study by every fraternity if the system as a whole is to play anything but a trivial role in the dynamic educational picture of the 1970s. ... Selectivity, Secrecy, and Service."

He called the first two "outworn trappings of a day that is dead," and the third topic "an important objective thwarted by a hedonistic wave," and one that fraternities needed to reclaim to survive as educationally credible institutions. Fraternities needed a reason to exist "besides the weekend party."

Advocating the value of more "heterogeneous groupings of abilities, backgrounds, and interests" within fraternities as "a far better educational preparation for life," Bill proposed the elimination of organized rushing and the resulting "typing" of chapter members.

"There is a place for secrecy at certain times and places in an open and free society," he continued. But "the existence of secret organizations cannot help but provide a focus for suspicion and misunderstanding." In handwritten notes for his speech to the Phi Kappa Theta convention, he was less circumspect, writing, "Secrecy will kill us."

The pledge period, he noted in his speech outline, is "so bad" and "the sickest part of the fraternity system." It is "incredible," he wrote, that "one man can assume superiority" over another. "Humiliation, persecution of pledges" goes against the philosophy of charity that lies at the heart of fraternal organizations. He proposed a junior brother-senior brother partnership to replace pre-initiation hazing.

"Abusing the bodies and minds of young pledges so they can join as 'brothers' is not a paradox, it is just plain SICK," he wrote. "Psychological hazing, through the charade some chapters use, is every bit as anti-intellectual as physical hazing, for it indicates becoming a brother must be associated with a hoax."

Formal rituals are a "beautiful concept," he noted, and if acceptance into fraternity membership is a proud moment, as he argued in *Tech News*, then that event should be witnessed by families and friends as "at any important ceremonial time in our lives." Secrets that "cannot stand exposure to light are intrinsically rotten," he noted in his speech outline, "like grubs hiding under rocks."

Service offers several ways for fraternities to make an exceptional contribution to college life, to the community, and to each other, Bill continued in his column. Fraternities, especially their dining halls, serve as a "natural media for faculty-student discussion." Weekly faculty guest programs could go a long way to improve connections outside the classroom and promote greater student understanding of both faculty and administration.

A renewed focus on community service could enable the fraternities "to permanently transcend the level of the annual Christmas party for orphans and the *Gazette* photographer." In his speech outline he described this as the "Alice in Wonderland gap," particularly on an urban campus, calling out the hypocrisy of fraternities' lack of social action.

Anticipating resistance to his calls for reform, Bill noted in his outline that "the most certain way to encourage drastic change is to try to resist it!" As he asserted in his speech, "We have reached our 80th annual convention. Whether or not we will be in session in a magnificent 100th anniversary convention rests to a very large extent on our ability to answer ... the questions of selectivity, secrecy, and service!"

The next 20 years saw many challenges, and although Bill had stepped back (to a degree) from involvement at the national level, he remained passionate about the changes required for long-term survival of his fraternity at WPI.

The Challenges of Change

"I think one of the great benefits of a fraternity, if it's run right, is the help that it gives these kids," said Jack Bresnahan, who served as president of WPI's Phi Kappa Theta chapter during his junior spring and senior fall semesters. He met Bill in the fall of his freshman year. Arriving on campus on a football scholarship, Bresnahan pledged at what was known as "the Catholic jock house." He remembers cleaning up the remnants of the house's Saturday night parties on Sunday afternoons, and "Bill would come marching in to help us get through our physics and calculus exams."

During his sophomore year, Bresnahan was house manager and it was a big job, he said. Phi Kappa Theta had grown to three houses by then, and they all had maintenance issues, including roofs to fix and mattresses and rugs to replace. Bill had to sign all the checks, so he and Bresnahan saw each other frequently. Even after Bill's wedding that January, Bresnahan would be invited over to the Grogan house to join in the dinners with friends visiting Worcester. "By the end of my sophomore year, I was meeting trustees," said Bresnahan. "We would all show up at Bill's house, cook steaks together, and solve the problems of the world."

Bill steered the student leaders through a few rough shoals. "He led by example," said Bresnahan. "He always gave great advice. He would nudge people in the right direction." Sometimes his nudges had to become more forceful lessons in leadership.

"In 1968, there was an incident on campus," Bresnahan recalled. "Five of our brothers were involved, at another fraternity. It happened on a Friday night, so of course it was all over campus by Saturday morning." Bresnahan and the fraternity's previous president "felt strongly that we wanted to do something, so we went to see Bill." Together, they resolved to "get the five out," but the large fraternity had many factions, and they weren't sure the members would vote out the troublemakers.

Bill drafted a letter from the Aquinas Association that told the members they would shut down the fraternity if they didn't expel the students involved. Association president Fran Harvey '37 signed the letter, giving Bresnahan the leverage he needed. "Sunday night at the house meeting, I said we had no choice," he reported, "and we voted them out." They had faced the problem head on, and with Bill's advice and counsel, managed it for the long-term health of the organization.

The next morning, "I was summoned to the president's office," he continued. A retired Army lieutenant general, President Harry Storke could be intimidating. "He looked at me and said, 'You have some brothers who have done a dishonorable thing, and I want to know what you're going to do about it.'"

"It was one of the best days of my life," said Bresnahan, smiling at the memory. "I informed the president, saying, 'We threw them out of the fraternity last night. They're not my problem anymore, they're your problem,' and I walked out." Three days later, he said, "I saw Storke across the campus and he said to me, 'I like you, you're a doer.'"

Despite their best efforts, the Phi Kappa Theta membership did not settle down as Bresnahan and the alumni advisors had hoped. And after he graduated, members continued to be drawn predominantly from the wrestling and football teams. But Bill Grogan remained a fixture at the house.

At a dinner for prospective pledges in the fall of 1967, Bill ended up sitting next to freshman Ron Zarrella, who remembers that first meeting quite clearly: "I had only been at school three or four weeks. Our conversation was so incredibly enjoyable I decided that was where I wanted to be." Zarrella acknowledged that part of the reason he was so impressed was that the "accomplished alumni at that dinner were pretty deferential to Bill."

When Zarrella changed majors to electrical engineering, Bill became his faculty advisor. And two years later, Zarrella was elected president of the fraternity to serve during the spring and fall semesters of 1970.

It was a tumultuous time. All fraternities were questioning their purpose in a period of social unrest and reassessment of past expectations. The difficulty in the early '70s was that fraternities no longer seemed relevant. Membership fell and some chapters closed. "People did not want to make a commitment," said Greg Stein.

At WPI, the fractious membership factions at Phi Kappa Theta had not improved relations with the alumni board, house rules were constantly questioned, the houses themselves were deteriorating, and the chapter needed some form of reconstruction. Out of concern for the chapter's future, the Aquinas Association held a meeting in May 1970, just a week after the student deaths at Kent State. Adding additional uncertainty to the role of fraternities in campus life was the proposed WPI Plan; no one knew what impact those far-reaching curricular changes could have on student housing decisions.

The alumni group reacted to the social chaos in the headlines with a calm, methodical process of self-examination and proposals for the future, not unlike the approach taken by the Plan's creators. Zarrella was one of five undergraduates who joined three alumni on a joint committee that took on the challenge of conducting a study and drafting three reports: one to describe the present status of the fraternity; a second to outline goals and objectives for the fraternity's future functions and alternative ways to achieve them; and a third to develop a specific plan of operation, either for ratification or further modification.

The detailed reports were completed in March and April 1971. The basic premise, according to the initial report, was to "look at the organization that causes the trouble rather than band-aid the troubles." It was an attempt to be "objective, honest, and present all points of view."

As the members of the Aquinas Association saw it, their role was to help guide the undergraduate fraternity members toward self-government, exercise its veto power if necessary, and "provide a focal point on which the wrath of undergraduates can be directed." Conflict was an acknowledged and inevitable result of the maturation process, and a way to "force both sides to consider more clearly the issues and consequences."

They recognized that much conflict surrounded the social rules of the house regarding student conduct and responsibility. To the alumni, the most popular officers were often not the best for governing the chapter, as they wanted students who could handle fiscal responsibility and plan for the continuity of the chapter.

For students, the rules that seemed appropriate in the 1950s and early '60s no longer suited this new generation. A fraternity should be a place to bring a date and let off pressure from intellectual studies. The rules set by the Aquinas Association seemed more restrictive than the ones students faced at home. Students rebelled against the requirement to sit down for formal meals, to clean, and to follow social rules deemed "particularly irritating." As the report noted, "there is a conflict between conformity and individual action." Sharing household duties created problems, there could be too much communication or too little, and a general lack of respect for the feelings of others was noted.

What to do next? Zarrella and his fellow committee members outlined the options, no doubt guided in large part by Bill Grogan. They suggested that the basic objective of Phi Kappa Theta was "to maintain a living environment that will enable a student to develop intellectually and socially. The relative attractiveness of this environment must be significantly better than those alternative living accommodations available to the student." Group living would foster mutual respect while embracing a wide range of individual personalities. Balancing group conformity with individual freedom could still deliver basic individual benefits.

The proposal admitted that undergraduates need to rebel against something. Rules, the report noted, "will be a source of conflict, regardless of what they are. ... Rules ... also serve a useful purpose at this stage in the maturation of a student. They form a convenient vehicle for conflict with authority, which is desirable in many ways. If confrontation with adults is not accomplished in this manner, it might be found in other, less desirable sources."

The organization had six options, the report said. It could remain as it is; become a stock company owned by member shareholders; be professionally managed; establish judiciary, legislative, and executive branches; become a commune; or become an honor society. While the fraternity could take its time debating how it wanted to be structured organizationally, its physical structure demanded more immediate action and would determine, in large part, the issues that Zarrella had to wrestle with as outgoing president.

Retaining its objective tone, the second report on the fraternity's future noted, "During the past several years, our living environment has deteriorated to the point that a decision for the future should be made." It continued, saying, "The blame may be unimportant, but the living conditions that contribute to the development of our students are vital. Our only reason for existence should be aimed at the intellectual, social, and moral development of the students with which we come in contact."

While Bill "loved vociferous debate," Zarrella said, the conversations resulting from the planning reports led to the closure of one of the fraternity's three houses and the departure of almost all its senior members, except those who were officers. Fewer rooms would be easier to maintain, and fewer members easier to manage.

"That was probably the most difficult time for me," Zarrella said. "What was tough was coming to the conclusion that there were people who just had to go to change the deteriorating culture. These were my friends. I grew up with them, but they had to go."

As he saw it, "Bill laid out a course, and then a course of debate with only one answer. It was hard for me to accept."

The third report offered an initial draft for what a future reincarnation of the chapter might look like; it would not be fully realized for another 35 years. Recommendations included creating an honor society–style chapter with only a few resident members. Full membership would be earned; it would not be automatic. Students interested in joining would start as affiliates, and then move into the house as associates on probation; only 20 or so would become full members—a high honor. Those full members would set the rules for conduct and take on more responsibilities for the house.

Despite all the troubles he wrestled with in his junior and senior years, Zarrella said he remained close to Bill, the fraternity, and his friends in the classes behind him. The changes they all undertook made a huge difference. He was gratified to see the chapter win the Founders Cup in

1972, a coveted recognition by the national fraternity organization as the best chapter in the country.

In 1979 Phi Kappa Theta honored Bill Grogan with its Distinguished Service Award. In his keynote address to the convention that year, he asserted his continued belief that fraternities remain important to college life. They offer fun and friendship, help students deal with the loneliness that is often part of college life, and improve retention rates, thanks to the built-in support system they provide, both academically and socially with a group of caring friends. Their traditions, the ones that give chapters their identities, bring a sense of community to individuals, and help students understand that they are a part of something larger than themselves.

During the years following the work of the joint committee, WPI's Lambda Chapter of Phi Kappa Theta benefited from a string of responsible officers. Bill would lead a Quo Vadis retreat for the chapter at the beginning of each new school year to discuss goals and community service ideas. Still, the transitory nature of undergraduate life meant that it would almost inevitably face another cycle of challenging behaviors from its members.

In mid-November 1990, a report of a sexual assault and underage drinking during a party at the chapter's main house on Institute Road, together with the "outrageous conduct of some members at a WPI–Coast Guard wrestling match," led to suspension of the chapter in late March 1991 for more than a year, as a letter to parents detailed. After requiring a majority of members to attend seminars on sexual assault and alcohol abuse awareness, WPI allowed the fraternity to reapply for recognition.

It received conditional approval in March 1992. Officers then attended training from Greek organizations and WPI's Student Life Office. The national office, having relocated to Indiana, became more involved with the chapter's activities. Phi Kappa Theta members renewed their participation in WPI's Interfraternity Council. In addition, WPI required that chapter leaders and alumni, along with representatives from the national office, attend a series of assessment meetings with campus officials. Full recognition was restored at the end of that year. News reports noted that the chapter planned to undertake renovations at the house on Wachusett Street that year and had plans to renovate the one on Institute Road during the following year.

"We stripped 17 coats of paint off 53 Wachusett," recalled Kirk Thomas, who headed the Aquinas Association from 1990 to 1992. But the chapter needed more than a fresh coat of paint to change its ways. The next decade saw a rising number of fights and underage drinking issues. Certain members of Phi Kappa Theta were not welcome at other fraternity parties. Andy Meier '00 had been a member of the wrestling team, and he praised the leadership his teammates provided for several years of the chapter's history. But after he graduated, he said, "they just couldn't lead themselves out of trouble."

As Bill wrote in a 2005 memo analyzing the situation, "The ghosts of the past doomed that effort. ... Kap should have stayed closed for at least FOUR years if we wanted to have a chance to really create a new, totally reformed chapter."

A New Chapter in a Long History

That chance came in October 2004. Amid issues of vandalism and disorderly conduct, the alumni board closed the house. The decision came during the break between terms. When some students learned of the decision, they retaliated.

"The treasurer tried to withdraw money from the chapter's bank account, but Bill had frozen the account in advance," recalled Len Dutram. "They threw furniture out windows and trashed the place." Residents had two months to find other housing.

Before the announcement, Bill, Pete Miraglia '95, and Adam Wilbur '06 had moved the official charter and chapter awards to Bill's basement for safekeeping. "People weren't going to be very happy," said Wilbur.

He and chapter president Shawn Gloster '05 were relieved at the closure. They no longer had to worry about what might happen over the weekend. As Wilbur said wryly, "We had a standing meeting every

Monday with the person in Student Affairs in charge of Greek Life to discuss what we'd try to prevent the following weekend."

Bill and other members of the Aquinas Association realized that now was the time for wholesale change. "A bunch of us alumni met at Bill's house," said Dutram. "We decided to wait it out, until those elements graduated." They waited out nearly a generation of students, until the previous members had all moved on. The goal was to close it, "to keep it, not kill it," as Bill noted later.

For the longstanding chapter advisor, "this was the opportunity to create his system—in a way he knew would work," said Nick Pelletier '09, who became the revitalized chapter's first president.

During the first year after the closure, Wilbur kept meeting and talking with Bill, sometimes in his office, sometimes in his living room. Should it remain a fraternity? Become a coed organization? Be modeled on the dinner clubs at Harvard? Over dinners, Bill hosted focus groups with students who hadn't joined a fraternity. After a great deal of research, including conversations with alumni of other fraternities, building inspectors, WPI trustees, administrators, and alumni, Bill drafted his recommendations for the future of Phi Kappa Theta at WPI.

"Today the institution of an entirely new concept of a fraternal organization is essential," he wrote. "A premature attempt at restoration of a traditional PKT will simply not be worth the time. If the next attempt fails, there will never be another chance. We MUST do it right and that will take patience."

Echoing the ideas formulated in 1971, the fraternity would no longer pledge freshmen. It would have a small membership, welcoming just 10 or so new members at a time. It would require members to have good academic records and diverse extracurricular interests. There would be no concentrations of students from any one activity, athletic or otherwise. There would be no pre-initiation hazing. Instead, there would be "a more appropriate bonding experience," such as "a pre-semester Outward Bound experience for all the members."

With fewer members, the chapter would no longer need two buildings. He outlined several options, including selling one to provide funds to remodel the other into "a first-class facility for meetings, meals, and socialization."

He concluded his memo by noting that it was his sincere belief that his recommendations "will lead us to the type of chapter which led the campus from 1950 to 1980. ... With creativity and alumni dedication, we can produce a new type of chapter of PKT at WPI with a new level of respect and prominence, which will again add enormously to the life experience of its members."

LEADING THROUGH INFLUENCE

While Bill remained "the idea guy at the head of it," as Wilbur explained, the alumni board refocused the fraternity around several pillars. "Some disagreements were more heated than others," said Wilbur, "but we eventually came out with a direction to go forward. Bill could oppose an idea one day, and then we'd reframe it and he would agree."

The new pillars included:

- Members would be engaged in leadership positions.
- No freshmen would be recruited, just upperclassmen.
- GPA of 3.0 or better
- No open parties in the basement
- No hazing; the chapter would operate as a "one class society" so that once someone was admitted, they would be on an equal standing with all other members.
- No "hell week" experience to force group bonding, but instead the entire chapter would travel outside Worcester to build for Habitat for Humanity in another community.

On whether or not to have a no alcohol policy, Bill felt he could not tell people not to drink, Wilbur related. So why not let the brothers decide? If it was their decision not to have alcohol in the house, Bill could be persuaded. "There was some shock, anxiety, and fear about this," said Pelletier. The decision to be a dry house, he said, would mean "it's on us

FRATERNITY HONORS CARDINAL

Pierre Cardinal Marie Gerlier, Primate of the Catholic Church in France and Archbishop of Lyon, as he was given an honorary membership in the Worcester Polytechnic Institute Chapter of Theta Kappa Phi, national Catholic fraternity, last night in the cardinal's suite in the Sheraton Hotel. The fraternity is an affiliate of Pax Romana, Catholic world secretariat of national university affiliations. In the picture from left, Thomas J. Coonan, III, Richard L. Tracy, president; G. Edward Desaulniers, Joseph E. Lemire, William R. Grogan, faculty adviser; and Cardinal Gerlier. Lemire is explaining the fraternity shield to the prelate.

ELECTED

As a young faculty advisor to his fraternity, Bill hatched the idea of making a visiting French cardinal an honorary member (*top*). He was well-known for his weekly "Me and Mike" talks (*above*). He later helped orchestrate the merger of Theta Kappa Phi and Phi Kappa to form Phi Kappa Theta and served as national president of the combined fraternity (*right*).

William R. Grogan of 10 Laconia road, above, has been elected national president of the Phi Kappa Theta Fraternity. Prof. Grogan has been a member of the national board of trustees of the national fraternity for Catholic men for 13 years. Prof. Grogan is a member of the electrical engineering faculty of Worcester Polytechnic Institute and is active in Newman Club work. The fraternity is represented by chapters at 55 colleges and universities throughout the United

163

Thirty-five years of service
Dean Grogan honored by Phi Kappa Theta

William R. Grogan, Dean of Undergraduate studies at WPI, was recently cited for thirty-five years of faithful service as chapter advisor to the Massachusetts Lambda chapter of Phi Kappa Theta.

The entire chapter was in attendance at a dinner reception held at the Sheraton-Lincoln Inn. Also present were alumni, faculty members, and distinguished guests from the national fraternity.

Brother Fran Harvey '37, acting as master of ceremonies, opened the evening by delivering a warm tribute to Dean Grogan, bringing back memories of some of the earlier days at the KAP.

Several guests from the national chapter gave kind words of thanks on behalf of Dean Grogan, who has also served as Phi Kappa Theta's first national president and executive director. National president Michael Duplantier, executive director Kirk Thomas, former president Robert Bailey, past executive director Robert Wilcox, Alumni vice president Roland Kraus, and administrative vice president Gregory Stein all expressed their appreciation to Dean Grogan for the endless hours he has devoted to his chapter and, as a symbol of that appreciation, Dean Grogran was presented a plaque honoring his thirty-five years of service.

Finally, those brothers who know Dean Grogan best, the alumni, honored their fellow brother. Three members of the alumni, each representing their decade here at WPI, spoke on some of the more humorous situations involving the Dean that have occurred over the years. Richard Lucey '55, Phillip Ryan '65, and Thomas Racey '72, all shared with us their experiences and memories of earlier days at the KAP with Dean Grogan.

To top off the evening, president Paul Dagle '82, representing the entire Massachusetts Lambda chapter, presented Dean Grogan with a Cross pen and pencil set, and Mrs. Grogan with a Phi Kappa Theta sweetheart pin. Dean and Mrs. Grogan were also given a four day vacation at the Trapp Lodge in Stowe, Vermont as a token of the gratitude and thanks that they have earned so well.

Bill joined the Lambda Chapter of what became Phi Kappa Theta as a WPI freshman in 1942, just seven years after it was chartered. In 1977 he was honored for 35 years of service to the chapter as a brother, advisor, and national leader (*right*).

THE TEⅢⅢⅢPLE
ΦΚΘ
OF PHI KAPPA THETA · An Educational Journal

FALL 2012
VOLUME 95
NUMBER 2
www.phikaps.org

A Man of Achievement

As William Grogan is honored at the 2012 Leadership Institute, we look back on the impact he has had on our Fraternity

The national organization of Phi Kappa Theta named Bill its Man of Achievement in 2012 and looked back on his contributions to the organization, locally and nationally, in a cover story in its magazine.

Welcome to the
William R. Grogan Chapter House
Our friend, mentor, and trusted advisor

Named in remembrance of his over six decades as Chapter Advisor
by the Aquinas Association on May 13th 2015

Bill's devotion to the Lambda Chapter over the course of 72 years
touched generations of brothers. They honored him in many
ways: inviting him to keynote the celebration of the chapter's 75th
anniversary (*top*), gathering in great numbers to send him off upon his
passing (*above*), and naming the chapter house for him in 2015 (*right*).

Bill met Mae Jeanne Kafer, a young widow living in New York, at a fraternity brother's wedding in 1961.

After a courtship of four years, he made plans to propose to her, as seen in a note in this calendar that he kept among his treasured mementos. They were married in the Lady Chapel of St. Patrick's Cathedral in Manhattan on January 29, 1966.

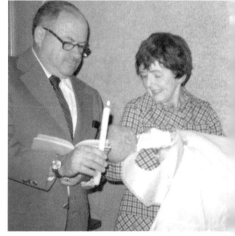

Bill and Mae lived in this house on Laconia Road in Worcester (*top*), which became home base for their travels, including skiing trips to Vermont (*left*), and a gathering place for family and friends, including neighbors Jack Bresnahan '68 and his wife Kathy, who asked the Grogans to be godparents to their youngest son, Matt (*right*).

Above: Bill kept a home office, which in later years was decorated with his many awards and honors. He remained devoted to Mae. Always petite, she became frail as her health declined in the 1980s. Mae's death just after Bill's retirement in 1990 left a void that was never completely filled.

Above: After his marriage to Mae, Bill's greatest joy was traveling. His many travel companions over the years included Mary and Bob Crook (*top*) and Pete Miraglia '95 (*left*, with Bill at the Great Wall of China). He enjoyed combining travel with visits to WPI's global project centers, including a stop at a center in Austria (*right*).

Bill's excursions covered large swaths of the globe, from
Ephesus, an ancient city in Turkey that he visited with frequent
traveling partner Terry Quinn (*top*), to St. Petersburg in Russia,
which he toured with Lance Schachterle (*bottom*).

Helsinki
Dear Carol
This is a lovely place. Very clean & open. The University is excellent & the reception great! Enjoying every thing immensely though working hard. Had reindeer tongue for dinner. Bill

Ms Carol Garofoli
Boynton Hall
WPI
100 Institute Rd
WORCESTER MA 01609
USA

PRIORITAIRE
PAR AVION

No matter where he traveled in his retirement years, Bill sent a postcard to his good friend Carol Garofoli.

SINGAPORE

Sir Stamford Raffles, Singapore's founder, surveys the city

Singapore
Hi Carol –
An absolutely fabulous city! The cleanest, friendliest and most efficient place on earth. You'd love it here. 80 miles from the Equator so its warm but quite bearable. Best to all! Bill

IMPACT
POSTCARDS

Ms Carol Garofoli
Boynton Hall
WPI
100 Institute Rd
WORCESTER MA
01609
USA

AIR MAIL

I can't believe I've landed in Red China!

The Traveler! Always visited! Nantucket, Iceland Canada and Shanghai, PRC

On a trip to Shanghai, Bill delighted at venturing into "Red China" and also adhered to one of his rules of travel: "never walk when you can ride."

G. H. HUPMAN, ORDNANCE manager—product development and design, left, gives Professor William R. Gro of Worcester Polytechnic Institute a share of GE stock in recognition of a patent filed jointly with Lewis H. VanBilliard Ordnance, who is accepting his stock share from O. D. Wertz, manager—support equipment, right. The patent covers a meth of controlling voltage in torpedoes by recirculating sea water.

GE's Van Billiard, WPI's Grogan Combine Forces to Receive Patent

A joint patent on a "process for the control of the electrical output of sea water batteries" has been issued to Lewis H. Van

IGE Officials Visit

International General Electric ficials from forty countries throu out the world will visit Pittsfi General Electric next week to a first-hand report on the operati

Bill's many awards and honors included a patent for a seawater battery innovation he co-invented for GE (*left*) and three WPI yearbooks that were dedicated to him: in 1963, 1983 (*below*), and 1991.

Dedication

Dean William Grogan

All of us know Dean William Robert Grogan. He has served WPI as a student, a professor, and a dean for nearly four decades. The list of his accomplishments, while at WPI, is indeed long and impressive. Perhaps anyone who dedicates his entire adult life to the education of youth could claim the same.

Certainly most schools, businesses, and other institutions have one or two loyal people who have given exceptional service. In this respect, WPI has been very lucky. Students, faculty, and alumni have all taken active roles to develop WPI and educate its students. However, few have committed the time and energy of Dean Grogan. He has accrued scientific and service awards illustrating his extraordinary devotion to his profession and his school. He is a former national president of the brotherhood of Phi Kappa Theta. But perhaps most important of all, he was the single most influential person during the implementation of the Plan, and he has dynamically led a constant effort to retain the quality of the Plan ever since, including recommendations this past year to upgrade the Plan. His work has had such results that this very school is a tribute to him and his colleagues who set the Plan in motion.

A good fifty years from now, Dean William Grogan will have faded into the relative obscurity of a Ralph Earle or an M. Lawrence Price, remembered perhaps only by a plaque on a wall or by a faint smile of a student's recollection. However, right now we have the opportunity to thank him for the time and devotion he has given to this school. With greatest admiration and love, this yearbook is dedicated to him.

The WPI Alumni Association honored Bill in 1974 with its Robert H.
Goddard Award for Professional Achievement, which was presented by
Paul Morgan (*bottom*), vice chairman of the WPI Board of Trustees.

Bill received (*clockwise from above*) the Chester F. Carlson Award in 1979 from the American Society for Engineering Education; WPI's first Trustees' Award for Outstanding Service from President Jon Strauss at Commencement in 1989; and the WPI Presidential Medal from board chairman William Marshall, center, and President Dennis Berkey in 2005.

Bill received the Goat's Head Award for Lifetime Commitment to WPI at Homecoming in 2012 (*top*). Afterward, he was congratulated by Phi Kappa Theta brothers from across the generations.

Clockwise from top: Bill with former students and lifelong friends:
Jim Demetry '58, professor emeritus of electrical and computer
engineering; Phil Ryan '65, chairman of the WPI Board of Trustees;
and Ron Zarrella '71, former board chair.

to provide more innovative programs." Each year, the brothers revisit the policy and take a vote.

They didn't wait to reopen quite as long as Bill had wanted. In the spring of 2007, the Aquinas Association identified three undergraduates to begin the "recolonization" process for the chapter. Wilbur had been president of the Student Government Association (SGA), and he recruited two other leaders from SGA for this initial group. They each went on to be SGA presidents. Bill did his share of recruiting as well. One of those student government members, Chuck Gammal '08, recalled a meal with Bill at Northworks and conversations about his future plans.

"He connects very well with you," Gammal said. "You can tell he wants to know who you are as a person. I was skeptical about the fraternity and its reputation. But the ideas that Bill shared excited me."

Between Wilbur and Grogan, Gammal was convinced. "He wasn't trying to sell—he was genuine," he said.

Pelletier had been a skeptic, as well. When he was approached the previous spring as a sophomore, he'd had no interest in fraternities. Persuaded by Wilbur to learn more, he came to his first meeting and realized how much he had to learn. He was soon speaking to groups about the new concept and was elected chapter president.

By the fall of 2007, there were 11 members who signed the refounding papers. Their first bonding experience was building a house in York, Pennsylvania, for Habitat for Humanity. "We slept in a church basement and cooked our own meals," said Pelletier. "Bill was really proud of this."

The founding members lived at 26 Institute Road, as the remodeling went on around them. "It was cold, the house had no kitchen and was barely livable," said Gammal. "And they paid to live there!" When the renovations were complete, however, the house had a full kitchen, eight rooms for up to 14 members, and a meeting room in the basement.

The chapter organized WPI's first Relay for Life fundraiser for the American Cancer Society and, as a small organization, recruited many other campus groups to help plan it. It was an overwhelming success, raising over $55,000. Now a WPI-wide event, it continues to break fundraising records.

More student leaders chose to join the reborn organization. Newcomers weren't called pledges, but in a nod to history, they were "friars." As the group coalesced and worked to establish the new fraternity, they inevitably hit impasses. "Bill was always around," said Pelletier, faithfully attending the Sunday night chapter meetings. "He would pipe up at the end of a meeting, offering his little words of wisdom" (see appendix). The chapter eventually grew to its natural capacity of about 35 members, with little growth expected beyond that level.

The revitalized chapter represented what Bill described as a "social innovation." In the fall 2007 chapter newsletter, he wrote, "a new Phi Kappa Theta has morphed into a highly selective fraternity of outstanding upperclassmen." His vision had become reality—"Bill had in his mind what it could be before anyone came on board," said Gammal. "We all bought into it and by the end, it was ours. We had ownership."

While not all alumni liked the changes, the Aquinas Association board insisted the fraternity was returning to what it had been before. They made a strong case, for by November 13, 2010, the date of the Phi Kappa Theta chapter's 75th anniversary, they had exceeded the goal they had set for a capital campaign among alumni, raising $430,000.

The brothers gathered at the Beechwood Inn in Worcester to celebrate, dine, and dance. Bill was asked to deliver the keynote address, and Zarrella introduced him.

Zarrella reflected on his advisor's accomplishments in securing approval of the WPI Plan from a fractious and politically charged faculty. As a junior at WPI, he'd watched Bill "one by one convince them that the change to what became the WPI Plan was not only good for WPI but would put it on the map for engineering education. ... I tell you, Niccolò Machiavelli had nothing on Bill Grogan when it came to that activity."

He then compared Bill's work on the Plan to his involvement with the chapter's reincarnation, and its "implications for Greek life, not only at WPI but possibly as a new model for the way fraternities and sororities should operate, should be constituted, and should be governed."

Standing at the podium, Bill represented all but seven years of the Lambda Chapter's entire history. He kept the audience of 150 spellbound as he spoke about the limits on Catholic student enrollment at WPI in the 1930s and '40s and the challenges all fraternities faced during World War II when their members were drafted or required to live on campus. He extolled the golden years, and mourned the nation's "deep malaise" during the Vietnam War and its aftermath.

The culture of drinking, drugs, and carousing that emerged had a lasting impact on fraternity membership. He noted how freshmen are just not ready to join a fraternity as there are too many other adjustments for them to deal with that first year. "And besides," he added, "their parents hated fraternities if they'd seen *Animal House*."

While he was proud to say "the Kap stands solid and secure in its new positive role," Bill was quick to warn the largest gathering of alumni in the chapter's history about complacency, turning to one of his often-repeated adages: "The top is a slippery place." He urged the next generation of members and alumni to avoid the temptation to cut corners. "Keeping standards is tough."

Bill Grogan was named Man of Achievement by the national organization in 2012, but an ear infection kept him from accepting the award in person in Providence. Instead, Gammal accepted the award on his behalf, and shared Bill's remarks with the audience.

The reinvented Kap continued to garner attention and recognition on a national level. "More chapters are responding to our model," said Pelletier. At the 2012 awards ceremony, the Lambda Chapter won the Founders Cup and every other award it qualified for.

"It was a little much," said Gammal. "The president of the house had to go up over and over again. He couldn't hold them all—we had multiple cars carrying them back to Worcester."

The proud chapter advisor sent a congratulatory email to the entire chapter for the diverse accomplishments "that brought the chapter the highest level of recognition ever received by a fraternity on the WPI campus. ... The chapter is at its highest level of achievement that I, for one, have ever seen!" He closed the email with a P.P.S. to offer some "closing advice to the triumphal members: Remember, guys, as I always said, the top is a slippery place!"

Even after the chapter was recolonized, Bill continued to think of ways to improve the experiences it provided to its members. He met Honduran native Jean Paul (J P) Miralda '13 at a Sunday chapter meeting and wanted to hear his ideas on how Kap could attract more international students. Fraternities offer the sense of home that many international students find missing at WPI, Bill noted, and their presence can help Americans better understand foreign cultures and traditions. He then peppered Miralda with questions. Miralda was impressed that Bill would ask his opinion and was still eager to learn. "The light bulb would go on and he would connect with his Italy experiences" in the Navy, he said.

This latest generation of brothers recognized they could learn much from the chapter's elder statesman. And Bill never tired of offering his advice and counsel. "The stories Bill would tell were worth hearing," said Wilbur.

In his last years, the entire chapter, some 30 to 35 men, would work together to bring him to chapter meetings, and faithfully pick him up from Briarwood to visit the Gold Star Diner for breakfast. That brotherly affection was his gift to them, Miralda said, as they learned how to care for someone who was their mentor and surrogate grandfather. The last chapter meeting Bill attended was at the end of D-Term in 2014 as the academic year drew to a close.

"The fraternity would not be here without Bill," said Wilbur. "It would have been closed a long time ago." Gammal agreed: "Bill had seen decades of ups and downs. He had perspective none of us had. His long-term view helped create something sustainable."

After Bill passed away in May 2015, the chapter's social media pages filled with images of Bill and notes from his brothers. With little debate, the Aquinas Association renamed 26 Institute Road the William R. Grogan Chapter House. And as Bill had requested, for the closing hymn at his funeral, the brothers of Phi Kappa Theta regaled their friend, mentor, and trusted advisor one last time with a hearty rendition of "Gaudeamus Igitur."

CHAPTER SEVEN

Creative Spirit, Agent of Change

Engineers solve problems—with constraints.

—Bill Grogan

WHENEVER BILL GROGAN joined an organization or a committee, or just took on a new task, you knew thoughtful change was in the air. He wasn't one to accept the status quo without questioning the case for maintaining it. His early Navy service gave him a breadth of experience he brought back to WPI in 1946. Before his 23rd birthday, Bill had encountered worlds well beyond his native Massachusetts, taken on new leadership responsibilities, and seen his electronics training applied to real-world situations. That clarity of vision later helped him see how, where, and what kind of changes might be needed—and, more realistically, what might be possible. Whether at WPI, GE, Bell Labs, or the Pentagon, his was a consultative approach.

On his return to WPI as a graduate student, instructor, and soon-to-be-faculty member, Bill would use a naval term to describe the school's approach to education: "dead in the water." WPI was then teaching a

Above: *As teacher of the year, Grogan led the WPI Commencement procession in 1969.*

traditional engineering curriculum in what he later called "an ossified fashion." Faculty members had little voice in the administration of the Institute; the department heads were in control. And there was little external push to change the way things were done.

It would take nearly 20 years before WPI's leadership would entertain the possibility of extensive curricular change, and when the first cracks appeared, Bill was ready to help the school evolve. During those intervening years, he fed his desire for change in other arenas, examining new approaches and responses to challenges in graduate education, continuing education, religious instruction, and even weapons design.

Bill stood apart in his determination to see change happen. "A lot of people have ideas," said Ron Zarrella '71. "But the number who can follow through and execute on them is very small." Bill was one of those people whose ideas really make an impact, he said. "He would provide the spark and see it implemented."

"He had a unique ability to put things together where others struggled," noted Zarrella, who had been a student of Bill's, a fraternity brother and officer, and later, chairman of the WPI Board of Trustees in the 1980s and '90s. As he sought to address issues facing the board, Zarrella often turned to Grogan for his perspective. "Bill often brought something a little different that no one else had—his influence and that mind of his."

Bob Fitzgerald '53, emeritus professor of civil and environmental engineering and fire protection engineering, also recognized this strength in his friend and colleague. "Bill was exceptionally orderly and systematic," he said. "Whether he was teaching, managing the WPI academic program, or mentoring an individual, he used the same approach." In his remarks at his friend's funeral, the retired professor and longtime fraternity brother explained how Bill celebrated the creativity of the engineer.

"He often noted that the work of a scientist is to develop knowledge and information," said Fitzgerald. "However, he would say, engineers solve problems—with constraints. The engineering process develops a solution in poorly understood and uncertain situations. The solutions must accommodate constraints such as time, money, politics, physical conditions, information, knowledge, and culture.

"Bill had an innate ability to identify the problem and recognize real constraints within the confusion (noise, as he called it). Then, he could address the real issues and guide a solution. He used this paradigm with people almost constantly. This was the core of his management style."

THE CHANGE AGENT IN ACTION

Just as business schools use case studies to illustrate the real-world challenges of managing people and organizations, the following six case studies from Bill's life serve to illustrate his engineering expertise, his management style, and his approach to engineering change in people, organizations, and technology.

CASE ONE: BUILDING A BETTER BATTERY AT GE

As a boy growing up in Lee, Bill knew that General Electric, in nearby Pittsfield, where his father and brother had worked at various times, was the area's biggest employer. So when he returned from his military service in late 1952, with his teaching schedule at WPI set for the following winter and spring, he applied for a summer job with GE. He reasoned that this work would build on his military electronics experience with the added bonus of allowing him to spend the summer break in Lee with his family. He would go on to spend every summer at GE until 1960.

He liked the challenge. He served as a consulting engineer and a project engineer for several Navy research projects, including the Atlas missile, the MK35 and MK44 torpedoes, and the Tartar missile guidance system. Although still only a summer worker, he joined GE's ordnance department in 1955 and served as sub-chairman for the guidance phase of the Atlas missile study group. In total, Bill produced 10 classified articles for GE's Technical Information Series, writing primarily about missile guidance and control.

Exhibiting what one manager at GE termed his "spirited curiosity," he then turned his focus to seawater batteries and GE's underwater ordnance development program. The batteries, which used salt water as the electrolyte to generate a steady current for several months at a time, had been developed by Dow Chemical and the Scripps Institution of Oceanography to power oceanographic instruments far out at sea. There was considerable interest in using these batteries in torpedoes, though the fact that their capacity was affected by changing water temperature and salinity levels seemed to limit their usefulness.

During the summer of 1957, Bill and Lewis Van Billiard, a product design engineer in GE's ordnance department, developed a method for recirculating seawater through the batteries, which would stabilize the temperature and salinity over time and help maintain a constant voltage. They built a working model and set up a test in ocean water that was witnessed by teams from Westinghouse Electric, the University of Washington, and the Applied Physics Laboratory of Johns Hopkins University.

GE published Grogan's technical paper "Seawater Battery Operational Characteristics in Torpedo Applications" in September 1958. The co-inventors filed a patent on their idea in late 1959, and patent number 3,012,087 was granted in 1960—and assigned to GE—for "a process for the control of the electrical output of seawater batteries."

At a May 1960 ceremony to herald the invention, George Hupman, GE's manager of ordnance product development and design, noted the fact that Bill's contribution "was made during a temporary summer work assignment adds greater significance to this achievement." Both inventors received shares of GE stock as a reward for their idea.

CASE TWO: CHANGING AN OUTDATED EDUCATIONAL CULTURE

Bill also used his summers at GE to stay abreast of emerging developments in the field of electrical engineering. In a lengthy July 1959 note to EE department chair Glen Richardson, he discussed a transistor circuit course offered to GE employees by RPI the previous winter, which was taken by "almost everyone" in his ordnance section. While he didn't explicitly suggest that WPI offer a similar course, his note about the RPI-supplied curriculum seemed designed to serve as a subtle nudge.

"I have an excellent assignment on a systems development project concerning control panels for a new ASW [anti-submarine warfare] weapon," he wrote. "Am up to my ears in transistors, diodes, and logic circuits. … It is amazing to see how obsolete vacuum tubes and relays have become—in fact, our contracts call for elimination of them in the entire system. … Vacuum tubes cannot be used under any circumstances!"

While the study of transistors had accelerated throughout the 1950s, electrical engineers did not have a clear understanding of solid-state systems based on semiconductor diodes and transistors. "There is still a lot of mystery surrounding all the new solid-state devices," Bill wrote, "and I'm sure their use would be avoided were it not for the fact the contract demands their use—and so [with a nod to GE's slogan at the time] *'progress becomes our most important product.'*"

Recognizing Bill's interests in curriculum development, Richardson asked him to upgrade the primary-level courses in electrical engineering taken by sophomores. One of those sophomores, Bradley McKenzie '58, later described how it "came as quite a shock to student nervous systems" to start "this transformation toward competent engineers as early as possible in the college curriculum." In addition to covering the basics, he said Professor Grogan required them to "utilize all stored knowledge (i.e., physics, mathematics, etc.) in associating the basics of electrical circuit theory with the practical world of interrelated systems."

In a letter recommending Bill for a 1960 summer institute on effective teaching, Richardson noted his role as a "leader in a group of young faculty who has made an extensive study of the factors affecting student motivation, and possible measures to be taken to improve the motivation of the undergraduate students." For Bill, altering the "ossified" approach to teaching would certainly be one way to encourage greater enthusiasm among students for their studies.

That summer institute for young engineering teachers, held on the campus of Pennsylvania State University, would create a ripple effect across WPI's campus when Bill returned, intent on putting a renewed focus on teaching quality. As intended by the program, he shared what he learned in Pennsylvania by mounting a number of memorable workshops. The first was for his fellow electrical engineering faculty members, but in the summer of 1964, just before classes began, he delivered a half-day seminar for the entire faculty.

"I've never seen a more excellent and practical approach to the everyday teaching of engineers," wrote Bill Roadstrum, professor of electrical engineering. "Although the experts in teaching theory that he brought in for the occasion were interesting and helpful, his own contribution to this meeting was ... the high point of the day."

CASE THREE: REORIENTING EDUCATION AT BELL LABS

A chance to examine how best to educate engineers, whether as undergraduates or as corporate employees, appealed to Bill's continuing interests and strengths. If the questions weren't being asked deeply enough at WPI, why not ask them elsewhere? He had the chance to raise those questions at Bell Telephone Labs.

"I got a job for Bill in the education department at Bell Labs for two summers," said his friend and fellow Navy man George Saltus '51, who at that point was working at Bell Labs in Whippany, N.J. After completing the spring semester's coursework in 1963, Bill moved south, becoming a summer housemate for George and his wife, Marilyn, in their home in Colts Neck, New Jersey, while he worked as a consultant for Bell Labs.

That first summer, Bill's job was to critique the lab's internal training program, Saltus remembered. Bell Labs wanted its employees to hold master's degrees in their fields, so it covered tuition for those who began working there without a master's. It also offered an extensive continuing education program beyond the master's level for employees who reached certain levels of management responsibility. For a brief period, Saltus, himself, taught a two-week course on management psychology.

Also that summer, Bill began a two-year study of more than 500 employees involved in external graduate education programs at 26 colleges and universities to identify problems and improve relationships between employees, their departments, and the schools. During his second year, he analyzed the company's advanced technology courses, making suggestions to bring the internal education program more in line with business objectives.

Grogan's detailed report, "A Study of Education at Bell Telephone Laboratories," appeared in a Bell Laboratories Service publication in September 1964. "An outstanding example of good organization and lucid exposition," Saltus said of the report soon after its publication. "His recommendations were so well thought of by our Committee on Education that many have already been put into effect."

CASE FOUR: EFFECTING CHANGE IN UNORTHODOX WAYS

Throughout the early 1960s, Bill and several of his younger colleagues in the electrical engineering department were frustrated in their efforts to promote innovation and a more contemporary view of education within their department, as Rick Vaz '79 recalled Bill's telling him. Despite the department chair's efforts to provide more professional development for Bill, it wasn't enough. Glen Richardson, who had held the job since 1958, was considered by the group to be "a very obstreperous department head" and resistant to change, Vaz said. The "young Turks" and Bill would meet, often at Bill's house, and discuss what they all wanted to do. Each time, "they would agree that Richardson was standing in the way of progress."

They took an unorthodox approach to changing the situation. Naming themselves the unofficial "Committee for the Professional Development of Glen Richardson," they set out to find him a new job. "They scoured the academic journals for job openings," Vaz said, "and they would submit his name. They would write flowery nominations of Glen Richardson for jobs at other universities." Eventually, the story went, their plan worked. Vaz continued, "One of those schools, having gotten the committee's nomination, contacted Richardson. He was intrigued, he interviewed, he got the job, and he left WPI. And in 1973 Harit Majmudar became the department head, much to the delight of everyone in the group."

Case Five: Steering the Navy to the Right Course

While his department head had not always taken his advice, Bill was pleased when the United States Navy asked for his counsel. In 1962 he began evaluating surface missile systems at the request of his former commander from the USS *Stoddard*, Eli Reich.

Grogan provided truly impartial assessments, no strings attached. This approach often set him apart. On his many trips to Washington, he would refuse to tell his Navy contacts where he was staying.

As Phi Kappa Theta executive director Bob Wilcox recalled, "He never went to dinner with prospective contractors. He didn't want to create any kind of relationship with them."

Although he was offered houses, cash, and even women to sway his opinion, Wilcox said, "Bill was not about to be a part of that. He wanted to give an honest opinion on who would give the best possible deal. So the Navy got a first-class, unbiased report from him."

His work on another committee also called for the distance and impartiality only a third party could provide. For an intense two-month period in late 1965, he chaired a committee tasked with the evaluation of the AN/SPG-59 radar system. After extensive deliberations with his committee of representatives from leading research organizations and corporations, they recommended that the government cut its losses and cease further investment in the project that involved more than $400 million.

"Professor Grogan's recommendations regarding the reassignment of technical resources and field equipment were subsequently accepted and implemented," added a note in his personnel file on his duties while a consultant to the Navy Department.

CASE SIX: PERSUADING THE CHURCH TO BLESS A NEW ORDER

Once Bill completed his consulting work for the nation, his attention turned to the church. A 1968 study of Catholic education commissioned by the National Conference of Catholic Bishops had recommended a more coordinated approach to instruction from elementary schools through college, including programming for adult continuing education. In mid-1969, the Reverend Bernard J. Flanagan, bishop of the Worcester Diocese, tapped Bill for a three-man study group that would take the first step toward restructuring every department involved with education programs in the diocese.

Bill and two local priests analyzed the administrative, educational, and financial aspects of existing programs. This core group then grew to more than 60 men and women from education, management, and business, who made up the Education Revision Study Committee. Along with its sub-committees, the study committee presented an overall action plan and a proposed organizational structure. As the *Catholic Free Press* reported in May 1971, the diocese's new Department of Education would have a nine-member policy-making Board of Education composed of the chairman of the advisory boards for each of the department's four divisions, plus five appointed individuals. Bill was one of those appointees.

The new structure, wrote Bishop Flanagan, promised greater flexibility, thanks to ongoing communication between advisory board members and staff; greater efficiency in use of personnel, facilities, and other resources; and greater economy, with the elimination of duplications in the system.

Bill went on to chair the Board of Education from 1974 to 1976 and served a second term on the board from 1993 to 1997.

THE PRINCE AND THE POLITICIAN: A CHANGE AGENT'S TOOLBOX

When Ron Zarrella was elected president of Bill's fraternity, Phi Kappa Theta, he asked Bill for some recommended reading on leadership.

The title Bill suggested took Zarrella by surprise: *The Prince*, Niccolò Machiavelli's 16th century classic on acquiring and maintaining political power. "He wasn't focused on the deviousness," Zarrella quickly added, "but on the genius of how to get things done."

"He was a scholar of the way people think," observed Bob Fitzgerald. "He was very sensitive to how you think, and he was very sensitive to how he thought you should think, and he found a way to change you."

Years later, Zarrella came to comprehend Bill's own 20th century adaptation of that 16th century advice. With Bill, people didn't feel manipulated. A self-described Irish politician at heart, he "had no degree in organizational management or organizational politics, but he had lots of experience," said Zarrella. "He was so good."

Those who knew Bill and worked with him on the many and varied projects he tackled in his career recall the diverse set of skills and management tools he could draw on to fit the need and the situation. As Zarrella has noted, this remarkable toolbox might have made Machiavelli, himself, take notice.

Tool One: Bridging Divides with Beer Diplomacy

"Bill Grogan was a very social being who thoroughly enjoyed working and interacting with people," observed Fitzgerald. "He could easily move from storytelling to giving advice to directing operations to expressing opinions on almost anything. He was as comfortable in a beer hall as he was as a major speaker at an international event."

Bill's approach to problem solving came down to the personal level. Practicing a form of beer diplomacy first learned at the Officers' Club during his Navy days, he often would separately invite two people who disagreed on an issue to join him for a brew at the Goat's Head Pub on campus.

They would arrive to talk with Bill and end up sharing a beer with the opposition. At that point, said Paula Delaney '75, who first met Bill when she was a freshman, "you're not talking to the dean; you're talking to Bill."

"A major skill was his ability to bring different points of view together to find out how much they had in common," said Fitzgerald. "He seemed to naturally listen, organize, and guide—and to make things happen."

Bill understood that communicating clearly also meant listening carefully. He considered it a vital part of the process of "bringing people along," said Zarrella. Recalling many conversations with Bill on the subject, Zarrella said he would explain, "Anybody who's part of the process should have the right to say whatever they want. You have to have the courtesy to listen to them. That's not to say that everybody's input will be part of the conclusion, but give them the opportunity to have their say, regardless of their level in the organization. Then make a decision and move on. Give people time to absorb that, then lay down the law, saying 'Here's where we're going and you need to get on the train.'"

TOOL TWO: REMAINING OPEN TO OPINIONS AND OPTIONS

Once you know who supports your vision and can help you execute it, Bill would say, you take it one step further. "If there are others who won't get on board, get them out of the organization," he would advise. "They won't ever change." Zarrella acknowledged that he had applied this approach to many management situations in his own corporate career.

"Bill Grogan was smarter than most people," said Willy Eggiman, retired professor of electrical engineering and one of the original "young Turks." In meetings, he said, "he was even-handed, congenial, and very fair about everybody's opinions. He wouldn't prefer one over another. He could talk to anybody."

Bill often sought multiple solutions. Having options, he felt, would keep the decision-making process moving forward, without the need to stop to find an alternative.

TOOL THREE: GIVING PEOPLE ROOM TO ACHIEVE

"Bill wasn't a micromanager," recalled Carol Garofoli, director of operations for WPI's Metal Processing Institute, who worked for Bill when he was dean of undergraduate studies. She said he would often leave it up to the people who reported to him to find their own solution. "He used to drop into my office once a week—I would never know when he was coming—and give me my assignments. And they were usually massive, from running new faculty orientation to taking on the summer school administration. I would develop the course offerings, put them in a brochure, and then manage the summer faculty payroll. I remember times when I would meet some of the exchange students at the top of West Street with pillows and sheets."

Times were different on campus in the 1970s, she explained. "In those days we never had an office like we have today. It was all done by a few individuals and very last minute." Bill would check in with her regularly, especially over lunch. "At least once a month we would have lunch at Club Maxine's," Garofoli said. "It was a great opportunity to have conversations about work and family. Bill always wanted to know how I was doing. It wasn't until Mae passed away that we become personal friends. Bill became a part of my family, and for every trip he took from then on he gave me his itinerary. I became his home base, and when his friends couldn't reach him they would always give me a call to see where he was."

TOOL FOUR: URGING PEOPLE TO FOLLOW A CLEAR VISION

"It came so naturally to Bill," said John Orr, the recently retired professor of electrical and computer engineering who was head of the department for 15 years, beginning in 1988, just two years before Bill's retirement. "He had a vision—he could help you see where things should go, and what should be there when you got there—and he helped you get there."

"He had an amazing ability to articulate a compelling vision. And the compelling vision was always tied very closely to the best interests of the students," said Rick Vaz. "And that's the kind of thing that's hard for most faculty members to argue with."

"He was able to see the way to get places," said Denise Rodino, who worked with Bill in her role as executive director for corporate and foundation relations. "He could see the future of what people were trying to do, even if they couldn't see it as well. He could see further than they could." She marveled at his ability to hone in on the important issues in a group discussion.

But Bill's vision was always backed up with data. As a "prime mover" on campus, "you knew he'd be in charge," said Frank DeFalco, emeritus professor of civil and environmental engineering, who was both a student of Bill's in the 1950s and a fellow faculty member from 1960 onward. "He knew everything; he had the data. No question bothered him. He was good."

"Bill was a prototypical electrical engineer," said Orr. "He was someone who was deeply knowledgeable and who understood the theory and could implement it, but who also understood the context in which it would be applied and used, which usually involved people. So he could navigate between the deep theory, the technical application, and the people involved. One of his areas of genius was to bring so many people along to become so passionate about the Plan."

As a former newspaper reporter himself, Bill wasn't above suggesting his ideas to the editor of the student newspaper, recalled Delaney. "Oh yes," she said, "particularly when they were talking about the Plan." But his influence preceded the Plan days. In one *Tech News* editorial in 1967, the writer noted that at Professor Grogan's request, they had held off responding to the Curriculum Study Committee's proposal, but as the faculty vote neared, they could wait no more.

TOOL FIVE: UNDERSTANDING YOUR AUTHORITY AND USING IT WISELY

When Bill was named dean of undergraduate studies in the spring of 1970, he was somewhat reluctant to leave the classroom world. Still, shifting roles from faculty member to administrator—a dean reporting directly to the president—would mean that his influence could be far wider. He soon realized that rather than helping individual students develop and grow (although he continued serving as an advisor to students well past his retirement), as a dean he could effect student development and growth on a systematic level. The deanship, "in a sense, becomes a lever," explained Vaz. "Your impact becomes greater."

While he had the title, he had few resources or official authority. "He didn't have a lot of money with which to bribe people to do things, and he also wasn't anybody's boss, except for a few administrative staff," said Vaz. "So he had to accomplish the whole thing through persuasion." Given his passion for the Plan and its expected long-term impact on WPI, Bill had a certain moral authority, Vaz said. He could call on his skills of "moral persuasion" to "convince people to become intrinsically motivated to further the WPI Plan.

"That was probably the one key attribute he had," continued Vaz, "that ability to win people over."

As registrar from 1986 to 1992, Delaney saw him in action, winning people over countless times. "He had such a nice manner that he could influence things" without drawing attention to his intentions, she said. "I would sit in these meetings and see things going south so fast," she recalled. The conversation would veer off topic or stray into areas of strong disagreement.

When things seemed to be going a little too far, she noted, "Bill would say, 'well, what about this?' and change the topic of conversation." As the meeting concluded, "he'd offer a summary of the discussion" that emphasized the direction in which he had wanted it to go. People would leave the meeting convinced that the solution they'd arrived at had been their idea. "It was instinctive," she said. "He wasn't even aware how dramatically he managed it."

"Sometimes," Fitzgerald added, "he was so skillful that he would summarize what had never even been brought up in the meeting, but everybody was convinced that it had been."

TOOL SIX: DEVELOPING A STRATEGY FOR MAKING CHANGE

Winning over converts to the new concepts of teaching inherent in the Plan was the first stage of Bill's advocacy work. As daily challenges inevitably arose, keeping that flame burning required another kind of campaign. In "Seven Steps to Sustainable Change at WPI," a 2003 article they co-authored for *Liberal Education,* the journal of the Association of American Colleges and Universities, Grogan and Vaz reflected on how to create changes on a college campus that would stick.

At WPI, they argued, giving an elected faculty committee the power to create a plan for change was an essential first step. That occurred in June 1969, when the Presidential Planning Group resigned and reconstituted itself with elected members. Gaining acceptance for the educational goals defined by that group was the second step. The faculty affirmed the goals for the Plan in December 1969. The third step outlined in the article was the institution of tenure and establishing a new governance structure, which gave faculty a voice in institutional decision making. At WPI, tenure preceded steps one and two, with the unanimous faculty vote in May 1968 and the trustees' adoption of tenure the following month.

Next came the advocacy work that Bill undertook so artfully to address ongoing opposition to the changes. "Those charged with implementing the changes at WPI never wavered in their belief that their program would be a success," the article recounted. "Even the most skeptical critics do not like to be left on shore when the ship leaves port."

Ongoing promotion of these changes in their formative years required the fifth step: having a consistent advocate and continuity in leadership. The General Implementation Committee, which Bill headed for more than a dozen years, always included a mixture of faculty committee chairs and academic administrators.

Recognizing that the ways to achieve educational goals may change over time, the sixth step was to allow those initial innovations to evolve and grow.

While the educational concepts remain, their delivery was modified, for example, by replacing the Competency Exam with distribution requirements. To ensure the successful implementation of these modifications—to institutionalize them—required the seventh step: accepting compromise.

TOOL SEVEN: NURTURING CHANGE TO MAKE IT LAST

For Bill, the creative implementation of the Plan led quite naturally to the creative institutionalization of the Plan. He realized that for the Plan to outlive his career at WPI, long as it was, there had to be more flexibility built into its structure.

"Bill very much understood the need for change," said Orr. "He could help everyone grow, change, and gradually evolve as the institution needed to evolve."

Once the massive curricular change was under way at WPI, Bill worked to protect the brand (although he wouldn't have described it that way). Details mattered. So did communication. Before classes began each fall, he would issue a memo to students outlining any changes that occurred at the school over the summer. The faculty would receive a similar memo, tailored to their interests and needs.

"On campus visits, he wanted to be careful who the students were who would lead the campus tours," recalled Delaney. During course registration, she said, Bill and then-dean of academic advising John van Alstyne "would be very, very careful about which kids would help other students make decisions on their courses. They knew how important that was."

And Bill understood, so well, how much perceptions mattered. "He might be scrambling, mentally, trying to figure out how he was going to do things," said Delaney, "but he approached everything with this quiet competence."

One ingenious approach he took, said Lance Schachterle, who worked closely with Bill as assistant dean of undergraduate studies, was to attend to every detail of someone's visit to WPI with great care, especially the Plan's advisory committee. After their meeting and dinner ended, each member of the blue-ribbon panel—leaders in higher education, engineering, and corporate America—would be paired with a "companion" to walk them back to their cars.

"Bill assigned me to walk with [Harvard professor of social change] David Riesman from Higgins House to the parking lot," Schachterle recalled. "He just told me that's what I'm supposed to do. He didn't tell me what to do, but he expected me to use those five or six minutes to stamp myself indelibly upon Riesman's memory. Riesman thrived on such opportunities. That's, in fact, what happened, though I certainly didn't realize that David Riesman would put me in his extremely large collection of academic contacts, but he, indeed, did."

"I only realized much later on how important it is to attend to the details like this," he said.

Bill also focused on the future more than the past. "He was always looking for the next big thing," said Zarrella, who has held senior management positions in several Fortune 500 companies. The globalization of WPI's education, encouraging students to undertake projects abroad, "may well be Bill's biggest contribution to WPI and to higher education," he continued. He saw Bill introducing ideas about global learning at a time when most students set their sights on careers with companies headquartered in the northeast United States. Today, Zarrella observed, "you can't work in a successful large, complicated company without having a very deep global perspective. You can't move up in management without it."

LESSONS LEARNED, INSIGHTS GAINED

As an administrator, Bill understood the human psyche. If there was good news to share, he would gladly invite the recipient to come to him. He did not want his office to be associated with the delivery of bad news, however, so when he had to disappoint someone he always went to that person's office with his message of misfortune. There was another practical reason for this approach, as he told Delaney—always have an exit strategy. Visiting their workspaces, she recounted, would mean "you can tell them the bad news and then leave."

When working for Bill, one's job description was "always broad, never specific," recalled Carol Garofoli. Her first job, education activities coordinator, actually involved editing the undergraduate course catalog and managing the winter Intersession program.

George Saltus also worked for Bill while he was a graduate student, running labs for him while he was away on Navy duty. Beyond basic guidelines, "he never told you what to do," Saltus said. Bill's philosophy was, "let the guy figure it out, and he'll do it better."

"He had a unique ability to be an authority figure at the same time that he was your best friend," said Bob Fitzgerald. "And that kind of a skill, to be able to maintain the authority when you need it and the camaraderie when you need it, and to be able to blend them, is a skill that I have seen in very few people."

Even as he became a senior-level administrator, Bill remained approachable. During registration, he would swap desks with his secretary so he would be in the hallway, available to answer any questions students might have as they went through the process in Boynton Hall.

"The methods Bill used to make the WPI Plan work is the model of what he did on a different scale with people," said Fitzgerald. Employing the Socratic method, he would ask leading questions but not tell them what to do. "Essentially, he helped them systematically solve their personal problems. He empowered them by helping them understand the situation, organize a solution, and sometimes bring in others to help."

"He loved everything about WPI," said Doris Horgan, executive assistant to dean of faculty Ray Bolz, "and if he didn't love something he would try to fix it."

People who knew him at nearly every stage of his life described him as straightforward, honest, caring, and willing to listen. "You felt Bill was always leveling with you, but not in an antagonistic way," said Orr. "He was passionate, and you might disagree, but you could see where he was coming from."

When faced with his ardent support for a specific position, most people understood that "Bill would sacrifice his own personal gain for a greater good, whether that was a person, a program, his fraternity, his church, or his country," concluded Fitzgerald.

His focus would remain on those changes deemed necessary to get things done. Bill understood, as he often said, that most change is glacial in nature. Ever the educator, Bill led not with a stick but with a carrot. His instincts told him that people are inspired to act by a deeply felt desire to improve: themselves, their organizations, and the world around them.

His greatest management tools were his wisdom, his energizing creativity, his boundless enthusiasm, his unyielding belief in the potential of the human spirit, and his endless supply of generosity and good will. Powered by these straightforward assets acquired through a lifetime of experiences, he sailed his ship of positive change, charting a future course of transformation and leaving in his wake a legacy of loyalty, admiration, and love.

A Remarkable Legacy of Leadership, Mentorship, and Friendship

It must be considered that there is nothing more difficult
to carry out, nor more doubtful of success, nor more dangerous
to handle, than to initiate a new order of things.

—Niccolò Machiavelli

MANY CLAIM THAT Bill Grogan was the most influential person in the history of WPI, or at least in the history of its most recent half-century. Many say it was Bill's educational vision and his remarkable leadership during the long and difficult implementation of the WPI Plan that saved the Institute. There is little doubt that WPI's admirable position today—with other colleges and universities looking to our university as a model for the future of higher education—rests solidly on the foundation that Bill and others began building more than 50 years ago.

That's when the Plan had its beginnings. It's also when I, then a civil engineering major at WPI, first met Bill. In those pre-Plan years I found WPI's curriculum uninteresting and uninspiring. I couldn't see how I would ever use much of what I was learning in the business career to which I aspired. Although I was receiving good grades, I considered leaving. As he would do so often through the years, and for so many people, Bill helped me think through my dilemma and chart the right course. Also, sensing that I was not alone in my frustration with WPI's rigid curriculum, Bill engaged me and other students as part of his search for a better way to educate scientists and engineers.

After a number of conversations with Bill and much reflection, I decided to complete my degree, go to work in industry, and then, when the time was right—when I had obtained solid business experience and was able to afford it—Bill would help me get into a top graduate business school. That is exactly what happened, and I will be forever grateful for Bill's guidance and friendship.

It was back then, during my student days, that I first realized how intensely interested Bill was in others. When he greeted you and asked how you were doing, it was never a throw-away line. He really wanted to know about you. And he often believed more strongly in you than you did in yourself. He strived to bring out the best in others, and he took great pride in their achievements. You always left an encounter with Bill feeling better about yourself, often having learned an important lesson and committed to improve. It's not surprising, then, that so many of us thought of Bill as our special friend.

This was because Bill understood the human condition. He could identify and manage feelings, emotions, motivations (his own and others), and he had an innate ability to use them to influence thinking, communication, and behavior—particularly in situations where conflict and stress might stand in the way of change. This is not a casual observation. It derives from more than fifty years of observing Bill in action as his mentee, his fraternity brother, and his close friend. Over that span, I developed a good understanding of who he was as a person—his style, intellect, personality, and approach—and how he led and interacted with others—in short, the qualities that enabled him to have such a wide-ranging impact in so many areas and in so many lives.

When I was appointed WPI's interim president in June 2013, Bill was among the first to congratulate me. He was 88 then, and although his health was declining, he maintained his connections and strong interest in WPI and our fraternity. Still my mentor, he met with me a number of times, often over long dinners, and shared his perspectives on higher education, WPI faculty/administration dynamics, the significant differences between undergraduate and graduate education, and the philosophical underpinnings of the Plan. He stressed how important it was for WPI to continue to experiment and evolve, and to never rest on its success ("the slope is slippery when you are at the top," he would say to me and to countless others). He wanted to be sure that WPI's next president would understand, appreciate, and be fully committed to further enhancing our distinctive undergraduate education.

Even in his later years, Bill still exhibited an extraordinary ability to lead and motivate others. At WPI, that ability stemmed from the respect, admiration, and trust he had earned with his faculty colleagues. They recognized him as a master teacher whose service beyond campus left an indelible mark: in the Navy, as a consulting engineer, and as an advisor to his fraternity. But Bill's well-developed leadership skills were also pivotal to his successes at WPI and elsewhere. Those skills were complex and multifaceted. They amalgamated beliefs and practices honed from hard-won experience with abilities that seemed almost instinctual. Everyone who knew and worked with Bill might have their own take on those skills. I offer mine.

He was a fair and honest broker of ideas. Whether he was helping fashion an innovative approach to learning, marshaling the WPI community to implement that program, or bringing two distinct cultures and traditions together to form a new fraternity, Bill believed in being inclusive, in soliciting input from a broad and representative cross-section of individuals, and in giving everyone an opportunity to express their viewpoints. With Bill it was never about his ego, but always about the vision, the cause, and the mission. His approach to leadership was open and transparent. But he also believed that being inclusive did not mean getting bogged down in endless debate. He was a decisive, persistent, persuasive, and inspiring leader with a bias for action.

He believed that his role was to help organizations—and people—move from today's reality toward a larger and preferred vision for tomorrow. For he knew that the greatest risk any organization or individual can take is to cling to the status quo within a changing external environment. Where others might feel satisfied with the state of things, Bill, with his endless curiosity, would ask: Why are things the way they are? How can we do things better? How can we create new value for our students, for our community, for higher education, and for our world? He was always looking to innovate, and people knew him as an overflowing font of ideas and possibilities.

When the time came to act, his decisions were principled. He always sought the appropriate and responsible path—the right thing to do. And he was not deterred by the naysayers who pushed back because a solution was just too hard, or the outcome too uncertain. Nor was he distracted or discouraged by barriers and setbacks. Instead, he could be patient and persistent, bringing others on board, building alliances, and attending to the myriad details required for successful implementation.

He was confident in his own ideas and abilities, but he was never conceited, boastful, or too proud or stubborn to consider and incorporate a better idea from someone else. Instead, he surrounded himself with like-minded people—bright, secure, curious, imaginative, ambitious, and passionately committed individuals who shared his drive to make things better. In fact, he sought them out, engaged them, energized them, and mentored them. They became his disciples.

Finally, we should not overlook the power of his personality. He was a generous spirit; he was truly selfless and kind, and he had a great heart. He was an exemplar of his Phi Kappa Theta fraternity motto: "Give, expecting nothing thereof." He was known for his wit and his warmth, and his gentle jests and gibes. He loved a lively exchange of ideas, he was a storyteller extraordinaire, and he had a flair for the theatrical, particularly when it would help him make an important point. And while Bill asked much of those he inspired, he always demanded more of himself. He had enormous energy and stamina. He seemed always to be juggling multiple projects, and with his intense focus, he kept all of those balls in the air. And in the end, he delivered impressive, long-lasting results.

Though Bill passed away in May 2015, those results live on, and his legacy endures: at WPI, at Phi Kappa Theta and other fraternities, and around the globe in the hearts, minds, and achievements of countless individuals whose lives he enriched. With little doubt, the most far-reaching aspect of Bill's legacy will be the impact his work continues to have on higher education. Bill knew that the WPI Plan was a model that could work beyond WPI's campus. He believed that the core principle of the Plan—its focus on learning by doing through applied, real-world projects—constituted the essence of a powerful approach to learning, one that could be effectively employed in any educational context. He became a relentless advocate for project-based learning, as an author, a speaker, and a leader within the engineering and liberal education communities.

I don't think Bill had many regrets, but the greatest may have been that the exquisite model he and other faculty members at WPI developed—and that he worked so hard to protect and improve over the decades—was not widely emulated by other colleges and universities. Perhaps, as WPI's 16th president Laurie Leshin noted in the introduction to *True to Plan*, the history of the last 50 years at WPI, the Plan was "so far ahead of its time that only now are so many other institutions realizing the power of the new type of learning environment that WPI built."

President Leshin joined the WPI family in June 2014, less than a year before Bill's death. I was with them during Alumni Weekend in 2014, the only occasion when they met. It was a time when Bill's memory was fading, but his vigor and enthusiasm for WPI were still much in evidence. I believe Bill sensed that his hopes for WPI's next president were more than fulfilled in Laurie. In fact, she not only embraced the Plan, but pledged to rally the WPI community behind efforts to make it even more effective and to win for WPI and the Plan the recognition that Bill knew they richly deserved. She launched a broad effort to develop a new strategic plan, drawing on the creativity of trustees, alumni, faculty and staff members, and students. The first objective in that plan is enhancing WPI's distinctive approach to undergraduate education—by helping each student chart a unique path through WPI, drawing on his or her strengths, passions, and interests, and by assuring that every student who wishes can make an impact at one of the more than 45 project centers in WPI's Global Projects Program, an initiative that Bill helped launch. The William R. Grogan '46 Endowed Global Projects Scholarship, established by Bill's friends and supported by WPI alumni, will help achieve the latter goal. I certainly would love to be an undergraduate at WPI today.

Another major goal of the strategic plan is to enhance WPI's reputation broadly, but particularly within the realm of higher education. Thanks to the legacy of Bill Grogan, that ambition is already being realized. In January 2016 the National Academy of Engineering announced that WPI would receive the Bernard M. Gordon Prize for Innovation in Engineering and Technology Education. Established in 2001 by Gordon—inventor, entrepreneur, philanthropist, and winner of the National Medal of Technology—the prize honors "new modalities and experiments in education that develop effective engineering leaders."

WPI was honored for creating "a project-based engineering curriculum developing leadership, innovative problem solving, interdisciplinary collaboration, and global competencies." The $500,000 prize is being shared by the university and four faculty members who have helped enrich the Plan and who readily acknowledge that they accepted the award on behalf of Dean Grogan and the legion of other faculty members, administrators, students, and alumni who helped build the Plan and made it what it is today.

More than any other honor it has received, the Gordon Prize has elevated WPI's visibility among its peers. But that recognition is just the beginning. With WPI's share of the prize funds it is supporting the creation and roll-out of the Center for Project-based Learning, an initiative aimed at realizing Bill Grogan's unfulfilled ambition to spread the benefits of project-based learning to colleges and universities across the nation and around the globe. Through the center, WPI faculty members who are steeped in experiential learning offer regular institutes on campus and travel to other campuses to deliver workshops. Like academic Johnny Appleseeds, our faculty members are spreading the seeds of a potent form of education, one that has been flourishing on the WPI campus for generations. And as project-based learning takes root across the landscape, WPI will be recognized as the place where it began.

While it would be difficult to imagine a more appropriate legacy for Bill Grogan, the fact is that he was probably most proud of the impact the

WPI Plan has had on its graduates. Today there are thousands of men and women who are leading rewarding lives and pursuing successful careers built, in large part, on the skills, sensibilities, and self-confidence they gained through their participation in the Plan. Thanks to a comprehensive study of those Plan graduates by the Donahue Institute at the University of Massachusetts, we know a great deal about how the Plan changes lives. The study, which consisted of a survey of 2,526 WPI alumni from the classes of 1974 through 2011 plus 20 in-depth interviews, examined the long-term professional and personal benefits of project-based learning at WPI.

It found that the Plan bolsters professional abilities (developing ideas, solving problems) and interpersonal and communication skills (being team players, taking leadership roles). It enhances graduates' professional advancement, increases their cultural and ethical awareness, and expands their world views. The Plan, the study found, also fosters personal growth, including the development of character and the ability to achieve a work/life balance. Many of these effects are stronger for women than for men. Clearly, the Plan produces the kinds of well-rounded, socially conscious, successful leaders that Bill always said it would.

Perhaps we should not find that too surprising, for the Plan, as we know it today, was very much the product of Bill's intellect, his belief in the power of education, and his remarkable leadership abilities. Over the course of his long and fruitful life, Bill solved a seemingly endless series of problems, from minor to monumental, as he created new value. In doing so, he transformed the lives of tens of thousands of people, in all walks of life, and in all corners of the globe. And through each of those individuals, whether they knew Bill as a teacher, a mentor, a brother, or a friend (including the truly fortunate, like myself, who knew him in all of those ways), Bill's memory and influence live on. For us, he will always be the presiding genius of the place.

Philip B. Ryan '65
Chairman, WPI Board of Trustees

Bill celebrated his WPI class's 62nd anniversary at Alumni Weekend in 2008.

The Wisdom of Bill

AT THE CONCLUSION of each Phi Kappa Theta Sunday night meeting, Bill Grogan would offer his fraternity brothers his "words of wisdom." Collectively, his advice came to be known as the "Me and Mike" talks, intended to help the fraternity's young members understand the expectations of the professional world.

As he explained, people who make decisions are sensitive to good grammar. For Bill, the most egregious grammatical error was misusing the word "me."

"Never start a sentence with 'me,'" he'd say. "You wouldn't say, 'Me went to the game,' so don't say, 'Me and Mike went to the game.' The correct version is, 'Mike and I went to the game.'"

On the use of "was" and "were," he'd say, "Remember, 'were' is for wishes. It's, 'I wish I were in Paris,' but, 'I was a hound dog.'"

Proper use of Latin terms still matters, he would say:

- A male graduate is an alumnus; multiple graduates (of either gender) are alumni.
- A female graduate is an alumna; more than one, alumnae.
- A piece of information is a datum; in volume, those bits become data.

Beyond the fraternity, he was never shy about sharing professional development advice with WPI students and other young people. Both classic and updated, they included:

- Be on time.
- Call if you'll be late.
- Send thank you notes; handwritten preferred.
- Dress professionally.
- Tattoos are a potential promotion killer.
- Don't let the waiter clear your plate if your dining companion is still eating.
- Be careful with Facebook (would you want your employer to see what is posted about you?).

As an academic advisor, Bill offered some counterintuitive advice: When studying, read the book last. Learn only as much as you need to solve the homework problems, then go back and read the book. In lecture courses, take good notes, transcribe your notes to relearn them, and *then* read the book to fill in what's important.

In the military, he learned one lesson the hard way. As Len Dutram '59 told the story, "One day Bill was in charge of the USS *Stoddard* as it steamed along with the Sixth Fleet. His order to the helmsman was, 'Left full rudder.' When the helmsman repeated the order, Bill replied, 'Right.' Soon he saw running lights looming to the right of their ship. They had almost cut across an aircraft carrier's bow.

"He was ordered to come see the admiral, who told him, 'You never say 'right.' Say, 'affirmative.' As a result," Len reported, "many hundreds of us will never say 'right,' but we'll always say 'affirmative.'"

During his time in the Navy, Bill also learned some important leadership lessons:

- Create an environment of mutual respect.
- Be honest and firm, and have consistent expectations.
- Give rewards where due, and keep punishment fair.
- Take care of your sailors—don't have favorites.
- Promote from within or your competitors will benefit.

Both as a faculty member and administrator, he adapted those military leadership concepts to the academic setting:

- Don't forget your friends; make good appointments.
- Loyalty counts.
- Bring students (and parents) into discussions.
- Be humble.
- Take people to lunch.
- Invite spouses to dinners.
- Ask your opponents for help.
- Get support from bigger players.
- Be positive about results.
- Show progress.

Bill's other key management maxims were "know your customer" and its corollary, "know the language and customs of your customer." To illustrate these points, Bill would act out a story with great vigor. As his colleague Lance Schachterle told it, "a dog food company spent infinite resources on scientifically designing a new dog food that met all of the laboratory parameters for nutrition. But, as Bill would say with a red face and pounding the desk, 'The damned dogs wouldn't eat it!' It had met all the scientific parameters, but it wasn't very tasty. The dogs just didn't like it.'"

"When Bill asked me to develop new global project sites in Europe and Asia," Schachterle said, he often said our students needed exposure to non-English speaking cultures because, "You can buy anything anywhere in the world if you know only English, but you can't sell anything to people if you don't know something about their language and culture." Others remember that as "Grogan's Law."

In the hiring process, he would apply what he called the "farm and paperboy theory" as a measure of success. Beyond other credentials and job experiences a job candidate might have, he would ask whether they had ever cared for a farm animal or had a paper route. A positive answer would boost their chances. His reasoning: If they ever had to be responsible enough to get up early to do a job, they were more likely to be successful in their career.

Truly big ideas will generate controversy, he told Rick Vaz '79. "If I ever had an idea that was big enough and bold enough to really make a difference," Vaz said, "I should know that some people were going to fight me." Proposing ideas that everybody agreed with was less impressive, he'd say, "because they probably weren't accomplishing much." If he wanted to make real change happen, he needed to understand that about a third of the people would fight him every step of the way.

Whether on the job or off the clock, Bill loved to travel the world. He had several pieces of advice for anyone planning a journey:

- Start your vacation on Thursday and return on a Tuesday or Wednesday.
- Take a few days to unwind, have a week to really relax, then give yourself a few days to let the worries creep back in.
- Never stand when you can sit.
- Never walk when you can ride.
- Never pass up the opportunity to use a bathroom.

WHILE I SPENT a pleasant afternoon with Bill Grogan in March 2014, I understood that as he neared his 90th birthday, the details of his life were beginning to slip away from him. So to gain a sharper sense of Bill throughout his life, I relied on interviews with close to four dozen of his friends and relatives who are listed below. Members of the book committee were among my key sources, and they also provided critical contact information which enabled me to reach many of Bill's contacts from multiple facets of his life. Most interviews were an hour or longer, and I gained so much from those conversations, both to capture the details of Bill's life and to understand his personality, his hopes and dreams, and his ever-present energy and sense of fun in most every task.

Martin Bertogg
Kathy and Jack Bresnahan '68
John Burgarella '50
Peter Christopher
Frank DeFalco '58
Paula Delaney '75*
Jim Demetry '58
Sean Donohue '93
Len Dutram '59
Willy and Mary-Louise
    Eggimann
Bob Fitzgerald '53*

Howard Freeman '40[+]
Chuck Gammal '08
Carol Garofoli*
Bill Grogan '46[+]
Kathy Grome
Charles Heventhal
Doris Horgan
Joan and Arthur Johnston
Tommy Larkin '16
Betty McNamara
Tom McNamara
Andy Meier '00

Pete Miraglia '95

Jean Paul (JP) Miralda '13

John Orr

Connie and Pete Ottowitz '58

Nick Pelletier '09

Terry Quinn

Denise Rodino

Phil Ryan '65*

George Saltus '51

Nick Scalera

Father Pete Scanlon+

Lance Schachterle

Greg Stein

Kirk Thomas

Bill Trask

Rick Vaz '79*

Steve Weininger

Adam Wilbur '06

Bob Wilcox

Ron Zarrella '71

*advisory committee member

+ deceased

Within a few years of retirement, Bill began to write a book on the Plan and his life in the years leading up to it. In an act of true friendship, Paula Delaney and Bob Fitzgerald supported him in this project by recording hours of his recollections, transcribing them, organizing them into subject areas, and mapping out ways for Bill to think through the topics. Many of the quotes from Bill were taken from these transcripts and and from drafts of his book. They provided a way to bring Bill's never-completed book to life through this project. I also received transcripts of interviews with Bill and Lance Schachterle by Jeffrey Cruikshank and John Landry for the WPI history project, which produced the worthy tome *True to Plan* in November 2015 at the conclusion of the university's 150th anniversary celebration.

The William R. Grogan Collection in the Curation, Preservation, and Archives department in WPI's Gordon Library was, quite literally, an enormous resource for this project. After Bill's death in May 2015, the archives received 53 boxes containing a true smorgasbord of his possessions. It was a banquet for a biographer, but the courses were served cafeteria style. Any given box might contain materials from his wife Mae's family, her diaries from their trips to Europe, travel brochures, copies of speeches, family letters, photographs (prints, negatives, and slides) and postcards. Working from a basic inventory provided by WPI Archives staff, I found he had saved dozens of letters sent to his family while he served abroad, yearbooks, course outlines, drafts and final documents from his years as an administrator, and endless ephemera that both prompted new lines of inquiry and generated occasional moments of astonishment. For example, in 1968 Bill was nominated for a Western Electric Fund Award for Excellence in Instruction of Engineering Students. While in the end he was not selected, the nomination materials that he saved among his papers painted a clear picture of his prowess and personality in teaching. Also helpful were multiple versions of his curriculum vitae, his personnel records from the U.S. Navy, as well as documents related to his tenure in the Electrical Engineering Department.

For context, some memorable quotes, and for general chronology on the Plan, I looked to Mike Dorsey's impressively comprehensive articles in the *WPI Journal*, "A Miracle at Worcester," and "The Best Laid Plans," published in October 1996 and Spring 1997 in connection with the Plan's 25th anniversary, and written when many of the key players were still living. Questions inevitably arose from the materials I found in Bill's collection, and back issues of *Tech News* and the *WPI Journal* from the 1940s through the 1980s, as well as the 100th anniversary history, *Two Towers*, the Plan's four reports (Two Towers I-IV), a transcript of the 1976 new faculty orientation regarding the Plan, and other university publications and committee reports provided the answers I needed.

To learn more about Lee, Massachusetts, and the surrounding communities, I found several local histories online, particularly William Clarke's *Early Lee School Houses*, Charles and Alexander Hyde's 1878 *Lee, The Centennial Celebration and Centennial History of the Town of Lee*, Amory Gale's 1854 *History of the Town of Lee*, and Berkshire Medical Center's booklet, "Our Story: A Brief History of Berkshire Medical Center," detailing the founding of St. Luke's Hospital. I also toured the Chambéry Inn in Lee, as it was once the St. Mary's School building, moved down the hill from the school's original site and restored as a bed and breakfast. Online copies of the *Berkshire Eagle* also filled in several gaps in my understanding of the Grogan family's milestones. In addition, online access to the *Brooklyn Eagle* proved useful in uncovering Mae's history.

For background on Bill's military experiences, copies of his correspondence regarding his leave of absence, documents on his promotion to lieutenant, records of the books he checked out from the USS *Stoddard's* library collection, his yearbooks from WPI (*Peddler*) and his midshipman school class yearbook (*Side Boy*), as well as reflections in the *WPI Journal* of on-campus military leaders provided many welcome details. *The New York Times* covered Bill's graduation from the last midshipman class at Columbia, and *Motor Boating's* March 1951 issue provided excellent background on the Underway Training Unit program he attended in California in 1946. Bill also preserved letters and memoranda regarding his work as a consultant for the Howard Research Corporation on missile systems and as chair of the AN/SPG-59 Advisory Board. To understand Bill's invention, I found an article on saltwater batteries in the November 1958 *Popular Mechanics*. I also found several online articles on the missile systems he worked on at GE and later evaluated for the Navy.

Bill had a habit of saving every newspaper article about himself, so I enjoyed his self-curated collection of articles from the *Telegram & Gazette* and its predecessor papers, *The Fitchburg Sentinel*, and the *Catholic Free Press*, as well as Phi Kappa Theta's national magazine, *The Temple*. More articles from that magazine were available online. A DVD of the fraternity's 75th anniversary celebration from 2010 provided a wonderful example of Bill's style of oratory. I learned more about Joe King's Rathskeller in the *New York Sunday Herald* of November 1955 and in a New York City Landmarks Preservation Commission report.

For more background on Theta Kappa Phi and Phi Kappa Theta through the years, I particularly relied on my interviews with Jack Bresnahan, Len Dutram, Bob Fitzgerald, Chuck Gammal, Tommy Larkin, Andy Meier, JP Miralda, Nick Pelletier, Nick Scalera, Greg Stein, Kirk Thomas, Adam Wilbur, Bob Wilcox, and Ron Zarrella.

There are many other sources I could have checked both in the WPI institutional archives and within the William R. Grogan Collection, but time constraints prevented extended research. While I made every effort to confirm the facts in this work, I accept all errors as my own.

―――――――――― ACKNOWLEDGEMENTS ――――――――

THIS PROJECT WOULD have been impossible without the close and consistent cooperation of the book committee assembled by Mike Dorsey, director of research communications, whose career at WPI as a professional writer and editor dates back far enough to have overlapped with Bill Grogan's last five years as a senior administrator.

Meeting for the first time in February 2014, the committee consisted of Paula Delaney '75, Mike Dorsey, Bob Fitzgerald '53, Carol Garofoli, Amy Morton, Phil Ryan '65, and Rick Vaz '79. Phil continued to promote the project, affirming Bill's legacy as advisor and mentor to thousands at every opportunity, Bob patiently explained to me past systems of faculty governance and all things military, and Carol was a wealth of information on how nearly every interview candidate was connected with Bill and how to reach them. Mike also deserves special thanks, as he served as my calm and wise advisor for those times when I came up against questionable content or conflicting stories. He also has been a brilliant editor of this manuscript.

I am convinced there's a special place in heaven for librarians, and the staff members in the Curation, Preservation, and Archives department in WPI's George C. Gordon Library were busy earning their wings throughout this book project. For their patience with my never-ending requests; their willingness to scan reams of documents, years of student newspaper issues, and dozens of photos; and their good cheer about the intersection of library hours with my tasks and deadlines, sincere thanks go to Lora Brueck, Jess Colati, Michael Kemezis, Tanya Lane, Kathy Markees, and their team of WPI students.

While he was not on the interview list, I thank Matt Runkle '11 for smoothing the way for me talk with a number of fraternity executives, all of whom quickly agreed to speak with me about Bill even over the winter holidays. Jared Kepron '16 made it possible for me to tour the William R. Grogan Chapter House although he couldn't be there, and Tommy Larkin '16 walked me through every floor, sharing lots of great background on recent residents and chapter history.

I am grateful as always for the tireless support of my husband, Peter Hansen, particularly as a sounding board on my latest discoveries from the archives and the direction my narrative was taking, and for his assistance with everything from genealogical research to meal preparation as this project swallowed up so many nights and weekends.

NOTE:

BG in this index stands for William R. "Bill" Grogan.

Names enclosed in quotation marks are nicknames and may have been used in the text to refer to the individual.

Page numbers in *italics* refer to images such as photographs, newspaper clippings, correspondence, and drawings.